TRANSPORT RECALLED
NORTH AND MID-WALES

Front cover: So much to recall in this summer Saturday image of Gloddaeth Avenue in Llandudno in July 1955. Smartly-dressed holidaymakers stroll past the Creams Tours office, some no doubt enticed by the range of trips being advertised on the blackboards, or the stylish Leyland Tiger with its heavily polished radiator. The pre-war SS Jaguar limousine, already over 20 years old, gives its passengers an air of one-upmanship. The Art Deco Odeon Theatre and Ballroom, opened in 1935 but demolished in the late 1980s, provides an imposing backdrop. But pride of place goes to L&CBER 'toastrack' car No 20, one of four delivered in 1920, as it heads for West Shore. This was the last season the 'racks' operated, with the tramway closing completely in March 1956. (*John McCann/Online Transport Archive*)

Title page: A remarkable view taken at Penrhyn Quarry one evening in August 1961. Men are ending their shift by descending the rope-hauled Ffridd incline on one of the special wagons fitted with foot boards and slatted longitudinal seats on both sides, movement being controlled by a travelling brakeman. Many working practices at the quarries of Penrhyn, Dinorwic and Dorothea had remained unchanged since the nineteenth century but were swept away in the 1960s. (*Ron Fisher*)

Back cover (top): The ex-GWR 'Manor' class 4-6-0s were synonymous with the Cambrian Coast line in the latter days of steam. Over a two-day period in August 1963, several were used for Royal Train movements along the line. Immaculately prepared 7827 *Lydham Manor* and 7828 *Odney Manor* were in charge of the train as it headed north from Aberdovey (Aberdyfi). (*Derek Penney*)

Back cover (bottom left): Fondly recalled are the vessels of the Liverpool & North Wales Steamship Company. During the summer, they would ply their trade between Liverpool and Llandudno with over 2,000 day-trippers aboard. From Llandudno, they would often then be used for a short cruise round the coast to Menai Bridge, where *St Tudno* is seen tied up shortly before a return sailing in 1956. Built on the Clyde in 1926, this popular vessel was scrapped in 1963, the year after the company had ceased all operations. (*Dermot Priestley/Online Transport Archive*)

Back cover (bottom right): Independent bus operators in the area could always be relied on to be running the unusual. Purple Motors of Bethesda were using this well-presented 1949 Crossley DD42 (actually on loan from Deiniolen Motors for many years) in October 1969, although the ex-Stratford Blue Leyland PS1 behind had already been withdrawn from service. The Crossley was sold in 1971 for intended preservation but is believed to have subsequently been scrapped. (*Alan Murray-Rust/Online Transport Archive*)

TRANSPORT RECALLED
NORTH AND MID-WALES

MARTIN JENKINS AND CHARLES ROBERTS

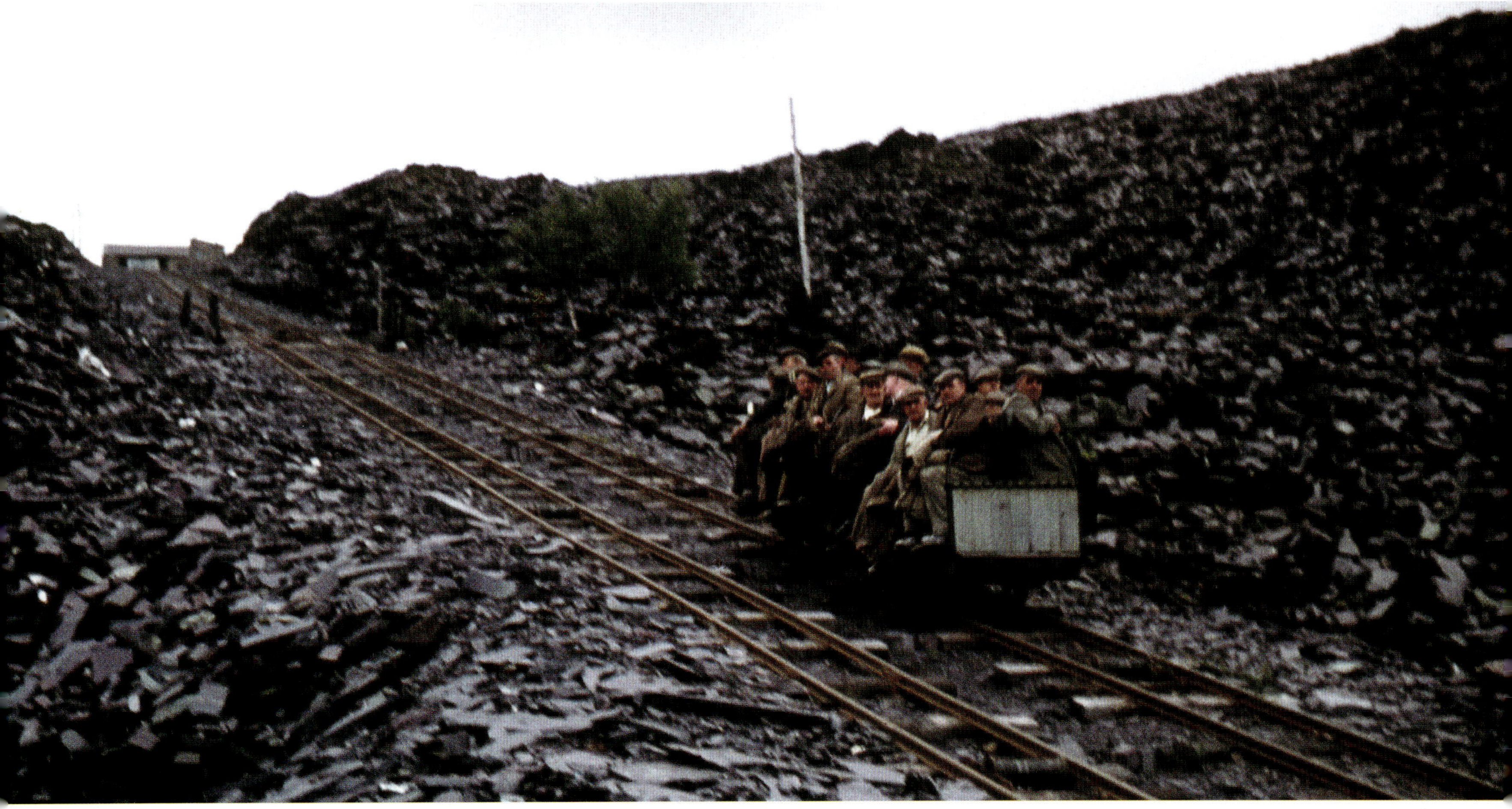

First published in Great Britain in 2022 by
Pen and Sword Transport
An imprint of
Pen & Sword Books Ltd.
Yorkshire - Philadelphia

Copyright © Martin Jenkins and Charles Roberts acting for and on behalf of Online Transport Archives Limited, 2022

ISBN 978 1 52678 707 1

The right of Martin Jenkins and Charles Roberts to be identified as Authors of this work has been asserted by them in accordance with the Copyright, Designs and Patents Act 1988.

A CIP catalogue record for this book is available from the British Library.

All rights reserved. No part of this book may be reproduced or transmitted in any form or by any means, electronic or mechanical including photocopying, recording or by any information storage and retrieval system, without permission from the Publisher in writing.

Typeset by SJmagic DESIGN SERVICES, India.

Printed and bound in India by Replika Press Pvt. Ltd.

Pen & Sword Books Ltd incorporates the imprints of Pen & Sword Books Archaeology, Atlas, Aviation, Battleground, Discovery, Family History, History, Maritime, Military, Naval, Politics, Railways, Select, Transport, True Crime, Fiction, Frontline Books, Leo Cooper, Praetorian Press, Seaforth Publishing, Wharncliffe and White Owl.

For a complete list of Pen & Sword titles please contact

PEN & SWORD BOOKS LIMITED
47 Church Street, Barnsley, South Yorkshire, S70 2AS, England
E-mail: enquiries@pen-and-sword.co.uk
Website: www.pen-and-sword.co.uk

or

PEN AND SWORD BOOKS
1950 Lawrence Rd, Havertown, PA 19083, USA
E-mail: Uspen-and-sword@casematepublishers.com
Website: www.penandswordbooks.com

Introduction

North and Mid-Wales, with their spectacular coastlines, dramatic hills and mountains, rolling countryside and farmland, and busy resorts and holiday camps, have always been popular tourist areas. Moreover, for the transport enthusiast during the years covered by this book, the area offered so much of interest: scenic main and branch line railways; quirky narrow-gauge survivors; remarkable industrial locations barely changed in over a century; canals, ports and harbours ranging from a major ferry centre to small freight facilities; tramways, electric and cable; plus all manner of connecting bus services, albeit infrequent in the more rural areas.

In this book, we take the reader on a journey in colour, covering the period from the mid-1950s to about 1980, trying to bring the area's transport scene to life. We are fortunate that a number of photographers were able to reach some of the more remote locations to record some fascinating views just before they were about to disappear. Without them, scenes of working quarries, their associated cableways and railways, and even some horse-powered operations, would not have existed and the content of this book significantly diminished. Our journey starts in Llandudno, where we arrive by steamer from Liverpool before heading east along the coast, south down the English border and cross-country to the Irish Sea. Heading north, we follow the Cambrian Coast and venture into Snowdonia. After a diversion onto Anglesey, we complete our circular tour back in Llandudno. En route, there are also plenty of diversions because that was the very nature of the adventurous transport enthusiast experience, never quite knowing what might be found just off the beaten track.

Thankfully, quite a lot of what survived into our period is now part of today's heritage industry, a vital component in the Welsh economy. The area has a bigger concentration of narrow gauge railways than anywhere else in the world. Through museums, visitors can experience the life of a quarryman or slate worker. The mainline railways still provide views of spectacular scenery, from the comfort of modern-day rolling stock, although most of the branch lines have gone. Buses and cable trams continue to take visitors to the top of the Great Orme. However, other gems are sadly missed: the Llandudno & Colwyn Bay electric trams; the Liverpool & North Wales steamships; and the many venerable buses squeezing down country lanes, often driven by their owner. Hopefully, this book will revive memories of what has gone, and also encourage people to visit the area to see what remains.

Just before this book went to press, news came that The Slate Landscape of North-West Wales had been added to the UNESCO World Heritage List, placing it alongside places like the Taj Mahal, the Great Wall of China and Stonehenge. The award recognises the role that this area has played to cultural and industrial heritage in Wales and the wider world. Many of the locations featured in the book, such as the quarries at Penrhyn, Dinorwic and Nantlle, and the Ffestiniog and Talyllyn Railways, fall within scope of the UNESCO award.

Both authors, with Welsh ancestry in part, have memories of the area stretching back into childhood.

All my early holidays were spent in North Wales. The train would take us from Birkenhead Woodside, usually with a change in Chester, and we would disembark in somewhere like Colwyn Bay with our cases, and trek to our booked accommodation. It was still quite a big adventure in the 1960s, rather than the swift car journey of today. The trams and steamers had gone by those days, but there were still the open top buses, ride-on miniature railways and, in my earliest memories, the sounds and smells of steam trains as they made their way along the coast. A memorable stay was in a holiday flatlet right alongside the Dyserth Branch – I think in 1966 – with a dirty, clanky 8F passing feet from the kitchen window going up the line every morning and back home again in the afternoon. In slightly later years, visiting all the Great Little Trains became a passion. It still is. (Charles)

My interest in North Wales transport began when I was evacuated in 1941 to Mold and then Rhyl. I remember riding Llandudno trams and having a 'tramtrum' when my mother wouldn't let me ride upstairs on a 'Bournemouth' during a downpour; visiting our home in Wallasey by train; taking all manner of buses to explore the countryside and finally waving down dimly-lit Crosville buses during the blackout with a tiny torch. In the 1950s, I rode and photographed the Llandudno-Colwyn Bay trams, visited the vast Crosville depot at Wrexham and started travelling on the local railways, especially the branch lines. In the 1960s, hours were spent recording the dying days of steam especially on The Cambrian. In the 1970s, we enjoyed idyllic family holidays at Arthog and then, in the late 1980s, my eldest daughter took her degree at Aberystwyth University. Regret: failing to pay sufficient attention to the quarry narrow gauge. Most unusual memory: playing King Lear in a student production at Caernarvon Castle in 1961 with steam whistles breaking the illusion. (Martin)

Place names

This book is set over a 40-year period where awareness of the importance of Welsh traditions and language was re-established, although place names on railway stations, bus destination blinds and road signs were often slow to catch up. In our captions, we have generally tried to use the appropriate spelling for the era of individual images, particularly where they match names visible in those pictures, but use present-day spellings when talking about current matters.

Acknowledgements

The authors would like to thank those photographers and collectors who have willingly made their images available, particularly Graham Jackson, Dennis Kerrison, Gavin Morrison, Alan Mortimer, John Ryan, Barry Shore and Dave Southern. Special thanks to the family of John Hobbs and to Ron Fisher and Sydney A. Leleux, not only for providing pictures, but also for having the foresight to take such evocative scenes of the Dorothea, Dinorwic and Penrhyn quarry workings. The authors should also like to thank John Pigott for providing detail for some of the quarry captions, Chris Poole for producing the map on page 7, and Nigel Bowker and Jonathan Cadwallader for checking the text.

The preservation of many images is secured through Online Transport Archive (OTA), a UK-based charity of which both authors are trustees. The book is a fund-raising initiative for the Archive, the authors having waived their fees and most of the contributors their right to image royalties. For more details about OTA, please visit its website (www.onlinetransportarchive.org).

Sources and bibliography

Most of the material presented in this book has emerged from personal recollections of many of the contributors supported by contemporary timetables, leaflets and booklets. Further facts have been obtained from, or verified against, publications by the Industrial Railway Society, Oakwood Press (particularly the work of J.I.C. Boyd), the PSV Circle, and from many other volumes dedicated to transport in the area covered.

Martin Jenkins
Walton-on-Thames

Charles Roberts
Upton, Wirral, April 2022

Dedication

This book is dedicated to the memory of Geoff Smith who was an acknowledged expert on all forms of Welsh transport as well as a superb photographer. He made an enormous input into this book, providing images, caption verification and personal memories.

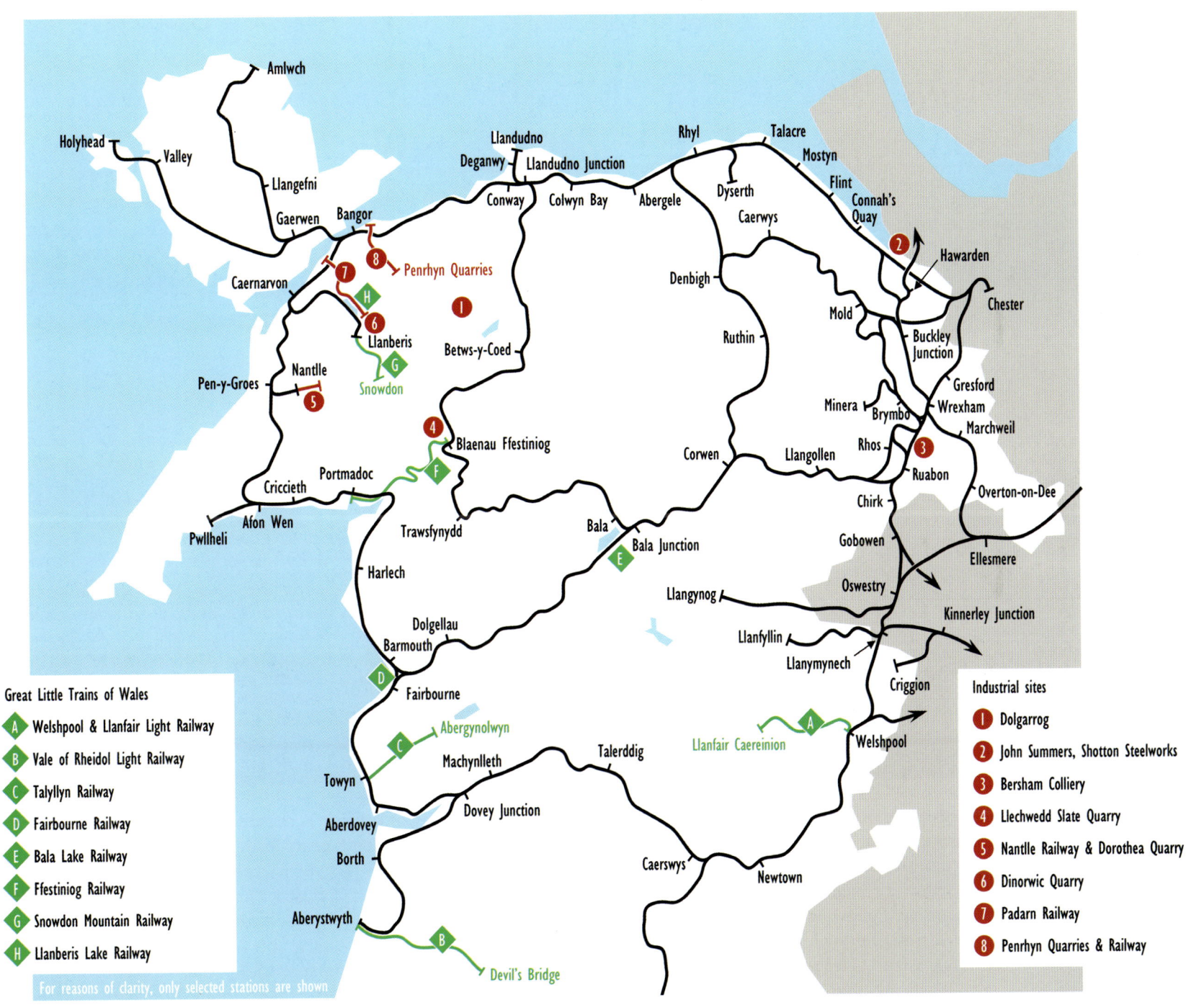

This transport journey through North and Mid-Wales begins and ends at Llandudno which is situated on a large curving bay flanked by giant limestone headlands known as the Great and Little Ormes. In the mid-nineteenth century, this small mining and fishing village was gradually transformed into a premier seaside resort with a wealth of amenities. Its fortune increased considerably with the coming of the railway which brought visitors in their thousands, especially from the northern industrial heartlands. Others arrived by coach, bus and steamship. Following a war-time break, the Liverpool & North Wales Steamship Company resumed operation in 1946, its fleet of three vessels offering Llandudno residents and visitors a comprehensive seasonal timetable of local cruises and longer distance sailings to Douglas and Liverpool. A regular on the latter was *St Tudno* (1926, 2,400 passengers). Looking resplendent with her flying bridge, two masts and raked yellow funnel, she is approaching Llandudno pier at the end of her 2 hour 20 minute journey from Liverpool on 9 July 1955. Excited crowds would have watched her arrival whilst others would be waiting to embark for a cruise to Menai Bridge. (*John McCann/Online Transport Archive*)

Visitors arriving in Llandudno in the mid-1950s were spoilt for choice. They could either ride up the Great Orme on one of the Corporation's quaint fleet of Guy single deck buses, which drummed up custom from a stand at the end of the pier, or on the Great Orme Tramway, which also reached the summit but rather more sedately. At nearby Palladium Corner was the Llandudno & Colwyn Bay Electric Railway (LCBER), a street tramway which went in one direction to the upmarket West Shore, and in the other towards Rhos-on-Sea and Colwyn Bay. (*R.L. Wilson/Online Transport Archive; Phil Tatt/Online Transport Archive; John McCann/Online Transport Archive*)

Many local people from the surrounding area arrived by bus. The all-pervading name throughout the area covered by this book is that of Crosville Motor Services. Such was its almost total dominance of the bus market that someone living in Merseyside and holidaying at one of the coastal resorts would, in all likelihood, have remained inside the company's operating territory. For the next 60 years or so, Crosville expanded relentlessly, primarily through the ruthless acquisition of smaller competitors. Having established a base in Llandudno, the company acquired three major businesses together with motley collections of vehicles which were gradually replaced by more standardised types, with Leylands predominating in the pre-war period. Typical was KA22, a 1937 TS7 with an Eastern Coachworks (ECW) body, seen here in Trinity Square, Llandudno before heading back to Conway (Conwy) in August 1957. The bus survived until sold for scrap in 1960, by which time it had become one of the last pre-war buses to remain in service. (Phil Tatt/Online Transport Archive)

Significant numbers of visitors also arrived by coach. On arrival, they could take advantage of the thriving market of local independent coach operators who offered excursions along the coast or into Snowdonia. As a result, the lucky photographer could often find all sorts of rare vehicles. Parked in a side street in 1957 is Hebble Motor Services (Halifax) Leyland PS1 14, whose chassis was new in 1947. Initially it carried a pre-war body transferred from a Leyland TS2, but this was replaced in 1952 by this full-fronted design by Windover of Huntingdon, oddly to 8ft width on a 7ft 6in wide chassis. The sticker in the window states that it was on hire to Cream's, the largest of the Llandudno-based operators, which implies it was running tours on their licence whilst based in the town for the week. The coach continued to run for Hebble until 1959 before seeing further service with other Yorkshire independents. (Phil Tatt/Online Transport Archive)

Few holiday-makers would have missed the chance to ride on the delightful LCBER, the seven and a half mile interurban to Colwyn Bay. With an eye for a bargain, the cash-strapped Company purchased a number of second-hand trams including ten open-top bogie cars (Nos 6-15) from Bournemouth in 1936. On the busy single track section linking Palladium Corner to West Shore there was just one passing loop and No 11 is seen here 9 July 1955 alongside 'toastrack' No 20. Note the summer white top on the driver's cap, the seasonal conductor in civilian clothes collecting fares on No 11, the rounded stop attached to the silver centre pole and the massive Odeon Theatre and Ballroom on the right. In good weather, the ride was idyllic but in the winter loadings were light with many locals preferring the competing Crosville buses. (*John McCann/Online Transport Archive*)

To replace their trams, the LCBER purchased a number of second-hand buses including 12 Guy Arab 5LWs from Southdown. In the first view, No 7 is outside Marks & Spencer on Mostyn Street. Dating from 1945, it had a 56-seat Weymann body with wooden seats on the upper deck. Behind the 'Red' bus, as they were known locally, is DLB980 one of a small batch of Bristol LD6Bs with 60-seat convertible open top ECW bodies delivered in 1959. Relations between Crosville and the Tramway Company were never cordial as each battled for traffic on the lucrative Colwyn Bay corridor. Ironically, when the trams finished, both parties did reach agreement over fares, scheduling and the provision of duplicates but to no avail. In fact, the situation deteriorated so much that each was in and out of the Traffic Commissioners' court until Crosville finally won the day when they purchased the Tramway Company for £40,000 in 1961. The second view taken on Mostyn Broadway on 17 May 1955 highlights the difference between the modern bus and the increasingly antiquated tram no 6, which dated from 1914 and was the only ex-Bournemouth car to be built by the United Electric Car Company. The 68-seater rode on Brill 22E maximum traction bogies and was scrapped in 1956. ML671 was an early Bristol Lodekka dating from 1954 with full-length radiator grille and mudguards, three-piece destination display, and cream band encircling the whole of the upper deck. In 1959, Crosville introduced a new route numbering system with area prefixes. (*Phil Tatt/Online Transport Archive; Ray DeGroote/Online Transport Archive*)

Following the opening in 1858 of a three-mile, double track branch from Llandudno Junction, thousands now reached the resort by rail. As traffic levels increased, the original Llandudno station was enlarged in 1892 to include five platforms, a wide carriage road and an overall roof. Eventually, a large area with some 20 sidings was needed to turn visiting locomotives and service carriage stock. In the first scene, Black Five 4-6-0 45248 waits to leave platform 3 in 1965, with a green-liveried DMU to the left. Since then, the station has been reduced with the loss of almost the entire roof, the elimination of all but three platforms and demolition of part of the frontage. In the second view, taken on 29 August 1976, 47088 *Samson* has just left the station at the head of a 12-coach train and is passing the carriage sidings already rusting through disuse. This Brush Type 4 was in traffic from July 1963 to September 2003. (*Photographer unknown/Colour-Rail.com; Barry Shore*)

One of the delights of the LCBER was the ride through Bodafon Fields where brambles, flowers and crops grew on each side of the line. Photographed from the top deck of another 'Bournemouth', fully-loaded No 14 is on route to Llandudno on 9 July 1955. To keep this isolated section clear of vegetation, staff armed with scythes were despatched from the depot. In good weather, everyone rode upstairs but, out of season, the handful of passengers huddled on longitudinal bench seats in the lower saloon. With no heaters, the crew would be heavily muffled against the cold. (*John McCann/Online Transport Archive*)

The most challenging part of the LCBER was the double track reservation carved into the side of Penrhyn Hill where the steepest part was 1-in-11. During the descent, drivers controlled the speed by skilful use of the brakes whilst conductors ensured the trolley stayed on the wire. On the ascent, drivers had to exercise caution to ensure they did not lose power, especially on wet and slippery rails. Problems could also occur in high winds. Lightly-loaded No 13 is about to pass the site of a siding which once served a quarry and stone-crushing plant. (John McCann/Online Transport Archive)

One of the great pleasures was a ride on one of the 'toastracks'. Built by English Electric, these four 60-seaters (19-22) were powered by two 37hp motors and had 14 full-width lift over bench seats and two half-width flip over seats either side of the trolley mast which also incorporated a large bull's eye light for night-time operation. Fares were collected by the conductor who balanced on the retractable running boards. With no bells or mirrors, the driver waited for two blasts from the conductor's whistle before moving off. No 20 is seen on the unmade road at St David's Corner on 9 July 1955. A few months later, the 'racks' went into winter storage, never to run again. (John McCann/Online Transport Archive)

Above: **Back on the** branch from Llandudno to Llandudno Junction, 70019 *Lightning* approaches Deganwy on 31 March 1963. This was one of the 55 'Britannia' 4-6-2 Pacifics which entered service in 1951-54. Unfortunately, these powerful locomotives enjoyed a relatively short life; for example, 70019 was only in traffic from June 1951 to March 1966. One well-remembered train to use the branch was The Manchester Clubman. From 1907 to 1942, the train had special carriages where 'regulars' had allotted seats complete with their preferred newspaper. This diagram was usually reserved for the best loco at Llandudno Junction motive power depot and was one of its last steam-hauled duties. (*Gavin Morrison*)

Right: **When the Llandudno** branch opened, a loco shed was built at Llandudno Junction. This had to be enlarged in 1880 and again in 1899 in order to service large numbers of visiting engines. Rebuilt 'Royal Scot' class 4-6-0, 46165 *The Ranger 12th London Regt.* is seen inside the shed awaiting repair on 22 June 1963. Built at Derby in 1930, it was withdrawn in November 1964. (*Gavin Morrison*)

The LCBER nerve-centre was at Rhos-on-Sea. The first view shows the company office and the second, No 17, one of the two surviving original cars. Built in 1907 by the Midland Railway & Carriage Company, Nos 1-14 rode on Mountain & Gibson equal-wheel bogies. Over the years, they were provided with double trolley poles, new controllers and less powerful motors. Some were also renumbered; for example, 17 had originally been 10. Although scheduled to perform the funeral obsequies, it was unfortunately involved in an accident. The third scene, taken inside the depot in 1960, shows No 3, one of the replacing buses, which had just been converted into an open-topper. Dating from 1945, it was ex-Southdown Guy Arab with a 56-seat Northern Counties body. The last 'Red' bus operated in May 1961. *(Phil Tatt/Online Transport Archive (above and right); John McCann/Online Transport Archive (top right))*

Returning to Llandudno Junction, D1848 heads an eastbound parcels on the up fast line on 17 July 1965. Having just emerged from Crewe Works, this Brush Type 4 is in two-tone green with yellow warning panel and four-character headcode. It was in traffic until April 1989. To provide much-needed extra capacity and improve running times, wherever possible, the line east from here towards Chester was quadrupled with the four-mile stretch to Colwyn Bay being completed in 1904. The Blaenau Ffestiniog branch can be seen trailing in from the left. This layout was simplified when the main line subsequently reverted to double track. (*Geoff Smith/Online Transport Archive*)

The 27-mile London & North Western Railway (L&NWR) branch to Blaenau Ffestiniog was opened in stages between 1863-1879 and was built to transport slate from the Blaenau quarries to a transhipment quay at Deganwy. Long after this traffic had ceased, a southbound Derby Lightweight DMU, with 'whiskers' at the front, is seen at Glan Conway station in 1961. Situated on the east bank of the river, it had a single platform station and a siding for agricultural produce and domestic coal deliveries. For a time, it housed a camping coach and there was even a resident Station Master until 1959. Listed for closure in the Beeching Report of 1963, the branch survived but this small station was axed in October 1964. However, in May 1970 it was reopened and then, ten years later, it adopted the Welsh spelling of Glan Conwy. (*Phil Tatt/Online Transport Archive*)

The remote nature of much of this area meant that surplus vehicles were often simply abandoned rather than being sent away for scrap. Furthermore, a ready market for old buses was created by land owners looking for cheap storage facilities. This example was found on a remote farm in the Conway Valley. Originally Crosville TA5, a 1948 AEC Regal III with Strachan 35-seat bodywork, it was part of a batch of 12 vehicles which the company was allocated by the state-owned British Transport Commission (BTC) when Bristol/ECW were unable to meet demand. Though non-standard, the batch remained in service until 1961, with TA5 being sold to a Territorial Army unit in Colwyn Bay. At a later date, it reached this farm and would eventually have rotted away had it not been removed by Quantock Motors, an operator of heritage bus services based in Somerset in about 2001. It was quickly restored to its original condition and continues to operate as a preserved vehicle. *(Roland Williams/Online Transport Archive)*

When introduced in 1933, camping coaches were an instant success and within two years some 200 were positioned at 160 stations across the country. During the war, some were put to other uses but, at the end of hostilities, they again proved popular especially as money was scarce. Rents were reasonable and the coaches usually well-appointed. This former Pullman lounge car, converted into a six-berth holiday home, arrived at Betws-y-Coed in 1960. However, as holiday patterns changed and more stations became unstaffed, the coaches suffered from neglect and rentals were phased out during the early 1970s. *(Phil Tatt/Online Transport Archive)*

Sometimes, organised school trips can provide unexpected benefits. Taking advantage of a visit to Dolgarrog Aluminium Works, Geoff Smith secured this precious view of the Company's 0-6-0 saddle tank on 10 July 1959. Built by Robert Stephenson & Hawthorns in 1943, it was used on a short branch to exchange sidings on the Conway Valley line. After the Second World War, traffic declined and the connection closed in 1960. On 31 July 1965, Geoff took another rare view this time of the Cowlyd Tramway, one of many narrow gauge mineral lines scattered around the mines and quarries of North Wales, some of which had been abandoned for years, with track and rolling stock often left to rust away. Built to convey men and materials to Llyn Cowlyd Reservoir near Trefriw, this 2ft gauge line was badly laid and poorly maintained. When Geoff walked the line, he remembers the track was 'deplorable'. At the top of the incline above Dolgarrog was a loco shed and outside were four wagons and what appears to be a contractor's four-wheel Ruston & Hornsby loco. The tramway closed following a derailment in 1968. (*Geoff Smith/Online Transport Archive (both)*)

Above: **Returning to the** valley, an early Derby Lightweight DMU is seen near Roman Bridge with a Llandudno bound train on 19 May 1964. Roman Bridge is the last station before southbound trains enter Ffestiniog Tunnel, which took four years to build and, at over two miles, is the longest single track tunnel in the UK. (*Geoff Smith/Online Transport Archive*)

Right: **Although the branch** line was an early convert to DMU operation, steam freight continued until 1966 mostly for domestic coal deliveries to Betws-y-Coed, Llanrwst and Blaenau Ffestiniog where ex-LMS Stanier 4-6-0 No 44866 is seen shunting wagons on 17 August 1966. Visible behind the loco tender is a nuclear flask and to the right are the remains of Oakley Quarry, once the largest slate quarry in the world. This grimy 'Black Five', which entered service in 1945, was withdrawn the following month. (*Geoff Smith/Online Transport Archive*)

In BR days, the Conway Valley Line trains terminated at the former L&NWR station, by then known as Blaenau Ffestiniog North, where a Cravens two-car DMU is seen in blue livery. A rake of cattle trucks, probably disused, are seen on the left. The branch escaped closure because it was to play a role in transporting nuclear waste flasks to and from a new power station at Trawsfynydd, for which the track was extended under the road bridge in the background to connect with the terminus of the former GWR branch. *(Richard Thompson/Online Transport Archive)*

From 1883, Blaenau was served from the south by a challenging single track line from Bala, the last section of which was built on the track bed of a former narrow gauge line. Latterly, trains took approximately an hour and a quarter for the 25-mile run including stops at all 13 intermediate stations and halts. On 30 March 1959, No 7428 waits to depart from the single platform terminus at Blaenau Ffestiniog Central, the suffix being a BR addition. The last passenger train departed on 2 January 1960 and the last goods train on 27 January 1961. When the connection between the former L&NWR and the GWR lines was completed in 1964, flask trains passed through here on the five-mile run to the special siding built to serve Trawsfynydd Power Station. In 1982, a new Blaenau Ffestiniog station was opened on this site, replacing the former L&NWR terminus and allowing direct interchange with the newly extended Ffestiniog Railway. *(Gavin Morrison)*

A six-car Metro-Cammell DMU formation on the Wirral Railway Circle Welshman Rail Tour of 22 March 1969 heads south from Blaenau on the former GWR line, with the mock Greek columns of the Tabernacle Calvinistic Methodist chapel prominent against the backdrop of hills and quarry workings. The chapel was demolished in 1974. (*Richard Thompson/Online Transport Archive*)

To transfer the nuclear flasks from road to rail, a siding was built behind the former Trawsfynydd Lake Halt. In the first view, a class 24 heads a flask train through the magnificent scenery on the first leg of its journey to the coast. When this traffic finally ended in 1998, the line was mothballed. A short distance south from the flask siding was Trawsfynydd station where, in the second view, the fireman replenishes the water tanks of No 7248 which still displays GWR on its side as late as 30 March 1959. The 11-mile journey from Bala included grades of 1-in-60 and took 45 minutes. Complete with passing place, Trawsfynydd had a loco shed and goods facilities. It also had a separate station for troops based at military camps in area. Goods traffic included slate, stone, coal, whisky, foodstuffs, agricultural and livestock requirements. South from here, the line did not die without a fight, but chances were scuppered by plans to flood part of the trackbed in order to create a reservoir. *(John Hobbs; Gavin Morrison)*

Back on the Holyhead-Chester mainline with a view of the four track approach to Llandudno Junction taken on 22 July 1962. This was when the Railway Correspondence & Travel Society (West Riding Branch) organised the 'Festiniog Scenic Rail Tour' which featured no less than six locomotives as well as a DMU which disgraced itself by derailing. The leg between Chester General and Llandudno Junction was worked in both directions by 46200, *The Princess Royal*. This was the first of a group of 13 LMS 4-6-2 'Princess Royal' Pacifics designed by William Stanier and introduced between 1933 and 1935 for express work on the West Coast mainline. Looking resplendent in its BR maroon livery with lining out, 46200 is seen on the down slow shortly before 12.15pm. All the 'Lizzies' were withdrawn by the end of the year. (*Derek Penney*)

Situated between Llandudno Junction and Colwyn Bay, Mochdre was the site of the world's first experimental water troughs installed by the L&NWR in 1860. These enabled speeding locos to scoop up water without having to stop. Having proved successful, the Mochdre troughs were re-sited at Aber near Bangor some ten years later. Just four months before going for scrap, rebuilt 'Royal Scot' 46155 *The Lancer* has a good head of steam as it powers eastward on the up fast line on 4 August 1964 close to the site of Mochdre and Pabo station, closed in 1931. (*John Worley/Online Transport Archive*)

In the early 1960s, the Railway Inspectorate was concerned that the weight of the huge transformers going to the new power station at Trawsfyndd could lead to problems if a steam loco broke down inside Ffestiniog tunnel or an outsize piece of machinery fouled its walls. This rare view taken on 7 May 1961 shows officials alongside D8038 which was to undertake the transfers. This English Electric Type 1 was in traffic from October 1959 to March 1976. In the background are the Arcadia Cinema and the taller General Post Office on Princes Drive, Colwyn Bay. (*Geoff Smith/Online Transport Archive*)

Returning to the LCBER, No 4 is seen on Penrhyn Avenue, Rhos-on-Sea on 17 May 1955. This was one of five single-deckers (Nos 1-5) purchased from Accrington Corporation in the early 1930s. Built by Brush between 1920 and 1922, two arrived as complete cars, their trucks being re-gauged from 4ft to 3ft 6in, whilst the other three, including No 4, came as bodies only and were mounted on trucks formerly under some of the Company's first generation trams. On the final day of operation, 24 March 1956, No 4 made the last trip from West Shore but when its controller developed a fault it was replaced by No 3. Although some residents opposed the abandonment, many were relieved to hear the last of the roaring and grinding on the worn-out rail.
(Ray DeGroote/Online Transport Archive)

Rhos-on-Sea was the western extremity of operation of Colwyn Bay Corporation, one of the smallest municipal bus operators in the British Isles. Services began in 1926 and the fleet reached a maximum of seven vehicles but had reduced significantly by the time the bus operation ceased in 1986. One of only two vehicles in stock at the end was Strachan-bodied Bedford VAS CUN302L, which was new in 1973 and seen here on 27 August 1979 on Marine Drive, Rhos. *(Michael J. Russell)*

When this view was taken on 27 August 1979, the trams had been gone for over 20 years. Intermittently, Crosville ran an open top bus service along a broadly similar route to the tramway. Working the M17 from Deganwy to Colwyn Bay, recently open-topped DFG68 has just turned off Rhos sea front onto the slightly elevated Caley Promenade. This is one of Crosville's 30 Bristol FSFs delivered in 1961/62, of which two were converted to open top in 1977 (DFG68/81), followed by a third (DFG72) in 1979. Painted in overall white livery with appropriate branding, they replaced the remaining Bristol-engined LDs from 1959. In converted form, the three FSFs remained in service until the end of the 1983 summer season. (*Michael J. Russell*)

On the approach to Colwyn Bay, the trams crossed the Chester-Holyhead mainline by means of Brompton Avenue bridge which, owing to its narrowness, had a single track used in both directions. Photographed on the occasion of an enthusiasts' tour on 17 June 1951, No 24 was one of a pair of all-metal, 56-seat streamlined cars built for Darwen Corporation by English Electric in 1936 and acquired in 1946. Known in their hometown as 'Queen Marys', their maximum traction trucks were regauged on arrival and the fleet numbers 23 and 24 transposed when repainted. The company hoped these luxury cars would persuade more residents to use the trams out of season but, unfortunately, the 'streamliners' proved something of a white elephant as the Ministry of Transport refused to allow them to carry passengers over Penrhyn Hill in case they toppled over during high winds. As a result, for a few years, they worked shuttles at either end of the line. This is the only known colour view of a 'Darwen' actually on the road. (*W.J. Wyse/ LRTA (London Area)/Online Transport Archive*)

Both these views were taken in Colwyn Bay on 9 July 1955. Heading east from Brompton Avenue Bridge, the trams ran along Conway Road through West End, with its elegant parade of local shops, some with sun blinds and others with more substantial iron and glass verandas. In the first view, the conductor is riding alongside the driver of No 9. Except for No 6, all the Bournemouth cars were built by Brush between 1921 and 1926, had two 40hp motors and rode on Brill 22E maximum traction bogies. The second scene is taken at the terminus. Here the conductor is in the middle of the road swinging the trolley on No 7 ready for the return journey. Such a manoeuvre could be quite hazardous, especially when the A55 was filled with holiday traffic. The road on the left led down to the station. Until 1930, the trams had continued beyond here to Old Colwyn. *(John McCann/Online Transport Archive (both))*

The coming of the railway transformed tiny Colwyn Bay into a popular resort with increasing numbers of prosperous businessmen living there but working in Chester, Liverpool and Manchester. Among the various attractions was a 10¼in gauge miniature railway. Opened by the council in the late 1940s, it passed into private hands in 1952. It ran for about 500 yards on a narrow strip of land on the promenade under the shadow of the main railway line. Passengers were push-pulled in very narrow coaches with sunshade roofs by live steam 4-6-0 *Prince Charles* which was built in 1949 by Carland Engineering of Harold Wood, Essex. This view was taken on 22 August 1968, a few years before this loco was replaced by a small diesel. The line eventually closed at the end of the 1986 season. *(John Ryan)*

Loading up outside Colwyn Bay pier in 1957 is one of the council's 20-seat Guy Wolfs, six of which entered the fleet between 1934 and 1948. The seasonal three-mile route to Rhos-on-Sea was generally operated by just two vehicles but, at peak holiday times, the entire fleet was sometimes pressed into service to provide a bus approximately every ten minutes. No 10 lasted in the fleet until 1960, clocking up an impressive 23 years of operation. *(Phil Tatt/Online Transport Archive)*

Between 1954 and 1960, Colwyn Bay's Guy Wolfs were replaced by five bonneted Bedfords, of which No 4, a Bedford J2LZ2 with a Spurling 21-seat body, is seen at the easternmost limit of the promenade drive on 21 August 1963. A quarry jetty can be seen in the distance, whilst on the right is the elevated Chester-Holyhead railway line. The 'Deckchair Station' sign is firmly fixed to the ground rather than being carried on the roof of the bus! (*Geoff Smith/Online Transport Archive*)

At its eastern edge, Colwyn Bay merges into Old Colwyn where, towards the end of crew operation in the area, Bristol Lodekka DFG186 is seen in typically heavy traffic on Abergele Road. Since demise of the LCBER, Crosville monopolised the lucrative Llandudno-Colwyn Bay-Rhyl corridor. With the growth in the use of private cars, the typical single carriageway roads were unable to cope, resulting in major bottlenecks at Queensferry, Llandudno Junction and Conway. Relief came through construction of the A55 expressway in the mid-1980s although this created a physical barrier between the Colwyn Bay/Old Colwyn conurbation and the shoreline. (*Roland Williams/Online Transport Archive*)

Colwyn Bay was a busy stop on the Chester-Holyhead line. In this view, Stanier 2-6-0 42967 has just left the station with a mixed goods including trucks carrying Irish cattle landed at Holyhead. The loco was of one of 40 modified Hughes/Fowler 'Crabs' designed by William Stanier and built in 1933/34. The station was later rebuilt to accommodate construction of the A55 expressway when goods traffic was also transferred to the new yard at Llandudno Junction. *(Richard Thompson collection/ Online Transport Archive)*

A jetty has existed at Llanddulas since the 1820s. Over the years, limestone from local quarries has been taken by ship to various UK iron smelting, cement and chemical works. In order to protect products awaiting transhipment during the Second World War a reinforced concrete structure known as the beach silo was opened in 1940. Then in 1947, the present jetty was constructed complete with a conveyor belt to bring limestone products from the quarry to the holds of the waiting ships via the beach silo. In the early 1980s, the jetty was further extended and is now the only one still operational on this stretch of coastline. Loading on 26 September 1960, is the ICI-owned *Cerium* (532GRT), built at Goole in 1943, and probably destined for their alkali factory at Burn Naze on the River Wyre in Lancashire. ICI sold the vessel to Canadian owners in 1965 and she was scuttled for use as a diving reef in British Columbia in 1991. *(Geoff Smith/Online Transport Archive)*

The station at Abergele opened in May 1848. When it was remodelled in 1883, the suffix 'and Pensarn' was added together with loops in both directions so expresses could overtake slower freight or stopping trains. These loops have since been removed. The section between Prestatyn and Llanddulas was quadrupled in the late 1890s and for some years a number of camping coaches were on site. In this mid-1970s view, Derby-built BR Type 2, 25041 is en route to Rhyl. Formerly D5191, it was in traffic for 20 years from May 1963 to May 1981. (*Richard Thompson/Online Transport Archive*)

Firm favourites with holidaymakers were Crosville's fleet of 'boats', six petrol-engined Leyland Lion LT3 single deckers which were new in 1931/32 but cut down to waist level in 1951 for seafront services and painted in the coach livery of cream, but with green trim. E52 was new in 1932 and originally carried fleet number 660. The entire E-class consisted of 75 vehicles with Leyland 32-seat, forward entrance bodies, which were fitted with perimeter seating during the war, apart from a small number which served as ambulances. Withdrawals took place during 1949-51 but the six 'boats' are believed to have lasted until the end of the 1957 summer season. This rare view was taken in the grounds of Gwrych Castle, a Grade I Listed nineteenth-century country house near Abergele, in the summer of 1954. Sadly, this attraction fell into disrepair, although it had a new lease of life when it hosted a TV 'reality' show in 2020. (*Phil Tatt/Online Transport Archive*)

Crosville's standard post-war single decker was the half-cab Bristol L-series with ECW rear-entrance bodywork, with a total of 254 entering service between 1946 and 1952. New in 1950, SLG188 (formerly KG188) was an LL5G, signifying that it was of increased length (30ft as opposed to 27ft 6in) and fitted with a Gardner 5-cylinder engine. It is passing the lodge of Bryngwenallt Hall, one time home of Lord Clwyd, on the outskirts of Abergele on route M1 from Rhyl to Llanrwst on 2 September 1964. Crosville was one of the last major operators to run this type, the final examples not succumbing until 1970, although SLG188 had been sold a couple of years earlier. (*Bryan Pyne/Online Transport Archive*)

A brief diversion now along the single track line linking Rhyl and Denbigh. Although closed to passengers in early 1953, it was used in both directions for eight more years by the highly popular summer season 'Radio Cruises' introduced by BR in 1951. The 'Cambrian Railway Cruise' undertook a clockwise loop, Llandudno-Rhyl-Denbigh-Corwen-Barmouth Junction-Afon Wen-Caernarvon and back along the coast to Llandudno. In its final season, which operated from 19 June to 25 August 1961, it left Llandudno at 9.45am and picked up passengers along the coast as far as Rhyl. After a 150-mile excursion through stunning scenery, the 'Cruise' arrived back at Llandudno just before 6pm, with one contented passenger claiming 'it was the most enjoyable journey I've ever made' – and all for £1/2/6d. Here, BR standard Class 4 2-6-0 75028 thunders through Trefnant station on 23 August passing the abandoned station and goods yard. Just days later, these trains were discontinued but those in the opposite direction continued until 8 September (see page 62). The section continued to be used by a weekday pick up freight until March 1968. (*John Ryan*)

The extremely rural nature of some Crosville routes is captured in this image of ECW-bodied Bristol LH6L SLL604 approaching the village of Nantglyn, some five miles south west of Denbigh on route M62. The LH was in production from 1967 until 1982 and Crosville bought two batches, one in 1969/70 and the one from which this vehicle came in 1975/76, as well as making some second-hand purchases. The majority were allocated to Welsh depots and were ideal for this sort of lightly-trafficked service. In the lead up to deregulation, Crosville was split in two under government direction in 1986, with Welsh operations (plus those from Oswestry) passing to a new company, Crosville Wales. Even with this type of one-man vehicle, revenue rarely covered costs and the company was heavily reliant on subsidy. (*Roland Williams/Online Transport Archive*)

In its heyday, Rhyl could be noisy and rumbustious when thousands, many from the industrial heartlands of Lancashire and Cheshire, came to enjoy the miles of sandy beaches, amusement arcades, variety shows and funfairs. As rail traffic increased, the section between Prestatyn and Llanddulas was quadrupled by 1897. At the same time, the original 1848 station was remodelled with through tracks, bay platforms, covered footbridge, two signal boxes, additional carriage sidings and enlarged goods yard, the work being completed by 1900. Seen on the down fast line on 29 August 1962 is Stanier 'Jubilee' class 4-6-0 45700 *Amethyst* (formerly *Britannia*). This engine emerged from Crewe in 1936 and was withdrawn in July 1964. Note the 0-6-0 'Jinty' shunting the yard on the right. (*Dennis Kerrison*)

Seen at Rhyl station on 21 August 1961 is 52119, one of the ex-Lancashire & Yorkshire class '27' which emerged from Horwich works between 1889 and 1918. This veteran 0-6-0 survived until October 1962. The second view depicts 'The Welsh Dragon', which provided a summer only, all-stations shuttle to and from Llandudno. Famous for being the only named push-pull train operated by BR, its loco and three non-corridor coaches carried appropriate name-boards. When introduced in the summer of 1951, it was, in some ways, a post-war version of the 1930s 'Sunny Sands Express'. Always well-used, it ran every day except Saturday, with some eight workings in each direction. It was usually hauled by an Ivatt Class 2MT tank engine motor-fitted for working push-pull trains, one of which 41276 is seen here. Built at Crewe in 1950, this 2-6-2 was in traffic until December 1963. For the reverse working, the driver's end of the push-pull formation also proudly displayed the name-board. Although operated by DMUs from 1957, 'The Welsh Dragon' unexpectedly reverted to steam for at least the 1962 season. The service was abandoned in the late 1960s. *(John Ryan; Dennis Kerrison)*

In this final view of rail activity at Rhyl, 44525, looks smart and clean as it shunts the sidings on the west side. This was one of a large fleet of 4F 0-6-0, first designed for the Midland Railway but subsequently adopted by the LMS as one of its standard freight engines with examples being built until 1940, this one being in traffic from 1928 until October 1966. As elsewhere on the coast, the station at Rhyl is now much reduced but the last of its two signal boxes was only decommissioned in 2018, although both are listed. The small loco shed closed on 11 February 1963. Although the spacious goods sidings were gradually reduced, by 1980 they were still visited by a daily freight mostly delivering coal. Today, some remain for use by engineers' trains. (*Dave Southern collection*)

The hub of Crosville's operation in Rhyl was the area immediately in front of the station, where a network of local and interurban services arrived and departed. This image shows DTO610, an all-Leyland PD2/1 which was new in 1949, from a batch of 17 which were reputedly a cancelled order for South Africa which was picked up by the BTC. The single piece destination aperture was very non-standard for Crosville and did not permit the route number to be displayed. Additionally, they were of highbridge design, with the upstairs gangway in the centre of the saloon resulting in a body height of 14ft 6in. This significantly limited their sphere of operation as so much Crosville territory was scattered with low bridges. The Art Deco Odeon cinema in the background dates from 1937 and is Grade II listed. (*Jack Barlow/Online Transport Archive*)

Just less than 20 years separate this view from the lower picture on the previous page, the location being the same but from a different angle. The vehicle is an ECW-bodied Bristol RE service bus, one of 183 delivered to Crosville in the period 1966-71, in addition to 66 of the high-floor coach variant. SRG166 was delivered in 1970 to the long wheelbase, 53-seat specification and was one of the last to be delivered with a flat windscreen and grille before a curved design was adopted by ECW later in the year. (*Roland Williams/Online Transport Archive*)

Crosville's 34 Weymann-bodied Leyland Tiger PS2s delivered in 1949/50 were handsomely appointed vehicles originally intended for sister BTC company Midland General. Fitted with higher-backed-seats than standard service buses, they passed through several phases during their Crosville career, including periods when they were in cream or green/cream livery for use on express or coaching work. However, when photographed turning from Elwy Street into Kinmel Street near the station in July 1964 on route M54 heading for Pensarn, STE927 (originally KA227) had been demoted back to bus work and all-green livery, albeit the chrome body mouldings hinted at more prestigious times. Three of these attractive vehicles have survived into preservation. The location is virtually unchanged today although, like many British seaside towns, Rhyl has struggled in recent years. (*Bryan Pyne/Online Transport Archive*)

One seasonal attraction still operational today is the Rhyl Marine Lake Miniature Railway which, as the title suggests, circumnavigates a large boating lake. Opened as early as 1911 it claims to be the oldest miniature railway in the UK. Built to the 15in gauge, it consists of a single unidirectional track just under a mile in length, a terminal station, locomotive shed and workshop. Its original general manager was Albert Barnes who also had a local locomotive building company at Albion Works which reputedly built six 4-4-2 'Atlantic' type locos for 15in gauge railways round Britain. There is much confusion over individual loco identities, but when this view was taken on 22 August 1968, *Michael,* thought to date from 1928, was one of four engines at Rhyl. Much of the coaching stock, mostly open bogie coaches each with five double seats, also came from the Albion Works. (*John Ryan*)

For many years, Crosville's popular and lucrative open top services linked the centre of Rhyl to holiday camps on the edge of town. Two batches of purpose-built convertible buses were delivered in the 1950s. The first were eight Bristol Lodekka LD6Gs delivered in May and June 1956 (MG811-818, later DLG811-818). They were broadly similar to standard service buses which were entering service at the time (see page 12) except for an additional chrome strip at cantrail level. In readiness for the season, the roofs were removed and replaced by open handrails. A revised design incorporating a small Perspex front shield was later adopted as shown in the image of DLG812 passing Rhyl Clock Tower (1948), on route to Robin Hood Camp. Six LDs which arrived in time for the 1959 summer season, differed by having Cave-Browne-Cave heaters, which accounted for the grilles either side of the destination display, and Bristol rather than Gardner engines. From this batch, DLB981 is seen outside the Queen's Hotel with a departure for Pensarn. The crew can be seen walking towards the vehicle in the background, wearing an unofficial uniform of a light green summer jacket and a pair of flared jeans. The view dates from the period when the NBC edict was that all service buses must be painted in standard fleet livery, although this was later relaxed with these open-toppers seeing out their final years in all-over white. (*Alan Mortimer/Online Transport Archive; Dennis Kerrison*)

Crosville's flagship North Wales route was the L1 'Cymru Coastliner', which provided an hourly limited stop service between Chester and Caernarvon (Caernarfon). Several generations of dual-purpose Bristol REs were employed, one of the earliest being ERG594 of 1966, which was one of just three vehicles in the fleet with this earliest design of grille and windscreen and is pictured in Rhyl still wearing its original cream livery. Subsequent repaints were into green and cream, and eventually NBC leaf green and white. ERG593-595 were the only bus-style Bristol REs in the fleet to have manual gearboxes and ended their days with the company at remote Mid-Wales depots or, in the case of ERG594, on school duties in Wirral. Following withdrawal in 1980, it had a period with a dancing troupe in Liverpool before being secured for preservation. (Dennis Kerrison)

Before the Second World War, Crosville had been almost exclusively a Leyland customer for its chassis requirements. M54 was a 1938 Leyland TD5 fitted with an ECW 52-seat lowbridge body. In this view at the terminus of Rhyl cross-town service 448 (later M91) at Weaverton, the arrangement of the upper deck seats can clearly be seen. When new, the vehicle had two small destination indicators, but these were replaced by the Tilling standard post-war style shown here. The lower blind, which included the route number and a series of via points, proved very cumbersome and quickly fell into disuse. Here, the blind information is supplemented by a 'Widd' board, a perspex panel which was displayed in the front lower deck window. The conductor is in his full winter uniform and equipped with a Setright ticket machine. M54 was withdrawn in 1959 and scrapped a couple of years later. (Dennis Kerrison)

Reflecting the high density of summer traffic, the coast line needed three different groups of water troughs, the ones just west of Prestatyn station being installed in 1885. Then 12 years later, when the line was quadrupled, all four tracks were equipped. On the approach, the fireman would spot the small, illuminated trackside boxes with the letter X which was a marker to lower the scoop whilst the driver kept to the maximum speed of 50mph. This view taken near the western limit of the troughs shows excess water spilling from 'Jubilee' class 45562 *Alberta* as it heads towards Llandudno Junction on the down fast line on 17 July 1965. With the end of the summer season and the continuing demise of steam, the troughs were last used in the September and removed the following year. Built by North British in 1934 and withdrawn in November 1967, *Alberta* was one of the last 'Jubilees' to remain in traffic. (Dennis Kerrison)

Enthusiasts were always on the lookout for the more unusual. With ex-LMS and BR classes tending to dominate the coast line, 'foreign' visitors were always a welcome addition. Probably working the Saturdays only 10.37am Sheffield Midland to Llandudno, ex-LNER class B1 4-6-0 61094 approaches the start of the water troughs located on the west side of Prestatyn station on 1 June 1963. Built by North British, this B1 entered traffic in 1946 and was withdrawn in June 1965. Note the Dyserth branch trailing in from the right as well as the signal box and goods yard. (Dennis Kerrison)

The single track branch to Dyserth was built to transport limestone and lead from the Talargoch mines near Meliden. Noted for its sharp curves and tough grades, trains to the quarry were propelled from the rear with strict speed limits being observed. Since its opening in 1869, the 2½ mile line had a chequered history. A passenger service, with five intermediate stops, ran from 1905 until 1930, but from 1951 to 1964 only coal was carried. However, a revived demand for lime for the steel industry led to introduction of a daily weekday goods transporting lime, crushed lime and limestone chippings, with steam giving way to diesel in 1966. This situation continued until September 1973 when the branch was closed to commercial traffic; the last movements involved the removal of redundant quarry material in 1974. The first view shows the quarry with a rake of empties waiting to be filled whilst the second shows a grimy Class 24 propelling a load of empties into the quarry sidings. (*Harry Evans/Online Transport Archive; John Hobbs*)

Dyserth was served by Crosville circular serves M35/M36. These two vehicles are laying over before taking their different routes back into Rhyl. On the right is DKA327, an ECW-bodied Bristol K fitted with an AEC engine. When new in March 1949, it was immediately loaned to London Transport, not reaching Crosville until early the following year. In order to achieve a vehicle height of below 14ft, the upper saloon featured a sunken gangway on the offside and bench seats accommodating four people. The vehicle remained in service until 1966 and then became one of a number of British double deckers to operate tourist services on the Canadian side of Niagara Falls, before reaching American owners in Detroit. The problem with vehicle height was solved to a large degree by the ingenious design of the Bristol/ECW Lodekka, whose offset driveshaft allowed centre aisles on each deck, eliminating the inconvenience of the sunken gangway, and with a vehicle height of only 13ft 5in, as exemplified by DLB825 on the left. The vehicle, a LD6B variant with a Bristol engine, was new in 1956 and served with Crosville until 1971. Note the imposing Dyserth Quarry workings in the background. (Dennis Kerrison)

Prestatyn became a major holiday centre following the arrival of the railway. Although listed for closure in the Beeching Report, the station remained open and these two views were taken in the early 1970s. As traffic increased, the original 1848 station, seen on the right in the second image, was replaced by an entirely new station as seen in the first view. When this opened in February 1897, as part of the programme to quadruple the track westwards towards Rhyl, it was unusual in having prefabricated buildings manufactured at Crewe. When the station was renovated in 1979, just one of these survived and is now Grade II Listed. Some of those alighting from the DMU on the down slow platform (abandoned in 1992) would probably be booked into the nearby holiday camp, originally developed as a joint venture between Thomas Cook and the LMS Railway. The two BR type 2 diesel locos in the second view are on the down fast. One is still in the two tone green livery whilst the second is in the later blue. In the far distance is the limit of the old four track section. By this time, the up slow had already been lifted and the semaphore display reduced. The gate In the bottom right corner led onto the down platform. Note the yellow BR lorry parked at the end of the cul-de-sac and the railway advertising board. (*Richard Thompson/Online Transport Archive (both)*)

In 1958, Leyland TS7 KA3 is seen outside the station waiting to transfer visitors to the town's large holiday camp. When new in 1936, this vehicle was fitted with an Eastern Counties 32-seat body but, like many in the fleet, the rigours of war took their toll and the bus received this 35-seat body from Anglesey-based Saunders in 1950. It served for a further 10 years, being 24 years old when finally disposed of by Crosville in 1960. It ran until 1965 for a travelling showman, typical major users of redundant buses in the post-war period. (*Bruce Jenkins*)

Having just passed over the railway by the station, DFG72 heads for Rhyl on coastal route M26 from Holywell via Mostyn. This is one of 241 F-series Lodekkas delivered between 1960 and 1968, the F indicating it had a flat floor in the lower saloon. This one is a relatively unusual FSF type, with a short wheelbase (S) and a forward entrance (F) and fitted with a Gardner 6LW engine. It was one of three of the batch deroofed in 1977/79 which ran until 1983 before open top services were converted to one-man operation. (*Dennis Kerrison*)

In a bid to reduce costs and improve running times, Beeching listed 18 stations between Holyhead and Chester for closure. Although some were well patronised during the summer, it was claimed loadings were too light during the rest of the year. The first view is of Talacre, one of the tranche of stations closed on 12 February 1966. Opened as late as 1903, it was essentially built to bring holiday-makers and day-trippers to the nearby beaches, sand dunes and burgeoning camp sites. Freight traffic ended in May 1964 but, right to the end, there was a good passenger service especially at peak times. The concrete panel platform still survives, and the signal box remained open until 2018. Here, a Metro-Cammell DMU is working an all stations to Chester on 21 January 1966. (*John Ryan*)

This view of the sidings at Mostyn was taken on 27 October 1980. 25267 and 25322 are hauling one of the last traditional coal trains before the introduction of Merry Go Round workings, from Point of Ayr colliery, which closed in 1996, to the ICI works at Northwich. These BR Type 2 locos emerged from Derby Works in 1966 and 1967 respectively, the former being withdrawn as early as February 1981, although the latter survived until March 1991 and is now preserved. The hopper wagons in the sidings were mostly used to transfer sulphur from Mostyn Dock to a chemical works at Amlwch. This section of the mainline was quadrupled in the late 1890s but reverted to double track in the mid-1980s. (*Dave Sallery / penmorfa.com*)

The origins of the modern port of Mostyn date back to 1822 when Thomas Telford completed a commission to construct wooden quays with rails for the transhipment of coal mined within the dock estate. Later, an iron works was also opened. This can be seen in the first view taken on 21 June 1966 shortly after it had closed. Also visible are railway wagons on the quay, a parked road trailer laden with bales of paper and three rail-borne cranes towering over the berthed vessel. In the second view, the coastal freighter, MV *Lady Sylvia* (1000 GRT) is navigating the channel leading into the docks on 3 August 1976. Built for German owners in 1965, it was sailing under a Cypriot flag in 1972 although beneficially owned by Thomas Watson of Rochester. When sold to other Cypriot owners in 1986, it was renamed *Tom G*. Very little traditional cargo now passes through Mostyn, but it has become a base for servicing the offshore wind farms in Liverpool Bay. (*John Ryan; Nigel Bowker*)

Several industrial premises along this part of the coast had their own internal fleets including Courtauld's, whose mills and works dominated the area. The company's predecessors had a presence in Flint from the mid-eighteenth century but when expansion was needed in the mid-1930s they established a new site at Greenfield, to the south-east of Mostyn. Outside the engine shed on 4 July 1965 were two of their Peckett tank engines, Nos 2 and 3 of 1938 and 1948 respectively. The older loco was scrapped on site in 1967 but the newer one was eventually secured for preservation and, after a rather nomadic existence, is now at the Stainmore Railway at Kirkby Stephen where it carries the name *F.C. Tingey*. Courtauld's were notorious for the pungent smells emanating from their plants which drifted over vast areas. (*John Ryan*)

Today, Flint is the only station still open between Prestatyn and Chester. The building on the down platform dates from the opening in 1848 and is designed in the Italianate style by Francis Thompson (no relation to the photographer) and is Grade II Listed. Next along the line was Connah's Quay, but this was another station to succumb to the Beeching axe on 12 February 1966. In the background is the power station which was built here in the mid-1950s because it was reasonably close to Point of Ayr colliery. After it closed in 1982 it was replaced by a gas-fired power station. The cooling towers were demolished in 1992. (*Richard Thompson/ Online Transport Archive; John Ryan*)

Crosville's depot at Flint existed primarily to provide vehicles for the nearby Shotton Steelworks. Posed on the forecourt is Bristol Lodekka LD6B DLB775 of 1955, which still sports the original design of grille, known as the 'Long Apron' and the three-aperture destination display which was fitted to all vehicles up to 1959, although the earlier ones subsequently had the top box panelled over. The bus was one of 12 transferred to sister NBC fleet Thames Valley in 1970, although this particular vehicle never actually entered service with them and ran for a number of years for an independent in Upminster, Essex. Allied to the major wind down of the steelworks, this depot closed in 1981, although the substantial building survived in industrial use until 2007 when it was demolished. *(Geoffrey Morant)*

In the days before food and drink services, not to mention toilets, were commonplace on coaches, the roadside 'halfway house' was an essential element of coaching infrastructure. Heading to and from North Wales, the Wayside Café at Bodelwyddan near St Asaph was always busy with arriving and departing coaches. The livery of XTA848 is that of Devon General subsidiary Grey Cars, but the lack of fleetnames and the slightly dishevelled appearance indicates it had already been sold as Grey Cars vehicles were always immaculate. When seen here on 18 October 1969, it was operating for Silver Star of Upper Llandwrog (see pages 137/138) and would have come from the Caernarvon area, so this break would have been much appreciated by passengers and driver – although the time allowed was hardly sufficient to queue for the loo and down a cup of tepid tea! The vehicle was a rare Beadle-Commer Rochester, new to Grey Cars fleet 1958 and running with Silver Star from 1966 until 1973. *(Alan Murray-Rust/Online Transport Archive)*

Despite Crosville's dominance in North and Mid-Wales, there remained pockets of independent stage carriage bus operation, one of which was Flintshire. A leading operator in this area was the family business of Phillips of Holywell. Founded in 1921, among their routes was one to Mold, which was latterly jointly operated with Crosville, whose share was given the route number B26. An interesting and varied fleet was operated, predominantly second-hand, including a number which had originated with Wallasey Corporation. CHF565 was a Leyland PD2, numbered 105 in the Wallasey fleet, which exemplified that municipality's habit of swapping vehicle bodies. The chassis was new in 1955, but the Burlingham 56-seat body dated from 1949 and had originally been on a 1936 Leyland TD4c when its original English Electric body was scrapped. It served with Phillips from 1965 to 1970 and is seen here on a short working of the Mold route heading for Halkyn on 8 March 1969. It was eventually secured for preservation and is now resident at the Wirral Transport Museum where restoration is well-advanced. (*R.L. Wilson/Online Transport Archive*)

Moving further east along the coast to Queensferry, which gets its name from the important boat crossings at this narrow part of the River Dee near the English border. For bus enthusiasts, the town will always be associated with the independent bus operator Hollis's Tours whose ex-Southport all-Leyland PD2 GFY410 is seen passing through Connah's Quay on a works service to Flint in August 1970. Proprietor Tom Hollis was a pioneer of the bus preservation movement from the early 1960s, rescuing a myriad of derelict buses from remote sites and storing them at his premises in Welsh Road, Queensferry. Although only a few were actually restored by him, his efforts ensured they were saved and many have been lovingly put back into original condition by subsequent owners. The company continued in business until the early 1990s. (*Bruce Jenkins*)

Among the larger employers in this area was John Summers whose iron and steel works supported a workforce of some 13,000 in its heyday. Following nationalisation in 1967, Summers faced falling demand caused by cheaper imports and the blast furnaces were silenced in 1980 although smaller-scale processing still takes place under Tata ownership. To handle heavy iron ore trains from the Birkenhead Docks, the former Great Central Railway (GCR) line from Bidston was upgraded in the 1950s and sidings laid at Shotwick where BR Standard Class 9F 2-10-0 No 92069 is seen on 16 April 1967 with 11 fully-laden wagons built by Charles Roberts (no relation to the author). Six months later, coupled pairs of BR Type 2 diesels took over these challenging workings. Summers' own locos moved the ore as well as limestone, oil, steel coils and coal from the sidings into the works and brought out completed steel products for onward transhipment. The company had a 2ft 6in gauge line as well as some 70 miles of standard gauge track. In the second view, No 23 is seen within the works complex in March 1970. This 0-6-0 built by Hunslet Engineering and acquired in 1958 to replace the last steam engines survived until 1977. The last remnants of the Summers' fleet were withdrawn in 1991. Today, part of the standard gauge is again operational. (E.V. Richards (both))

In spite of having its own railway station, Summers was not served by public bus services as it was located a mile from the Shotton-Queensferry road along a private drive. However, several dedicated contract services provided links from a bus station to surrounding towns at shift change times. Viewed from the railway platform, ex-Stockport all-Leyland PD2/1 DJA183, new in 1949, is seen on 27 June 1969. After serving in Stockport until 1968, it had a short period with the Potteries-based operator Berresford's of Cheddleton before reaching Ellis's of Buckley, for whom it was operating at the time. So vast was the area covered by the works, an internal fleet of lorries, vans and cars was required, hence the trio of red Morris Mini-Minors (left) carrying non-road-legal two-digit identification numbers. In the second view, some other non-road-legal vehicles can be seen including a pair of Ford D-series articulated tractor units as well as an ex-Accrington Leyland PD2. These were used to ferry employees from the bus station to other parts of the complex. (*John Ryan; J.G. Parkinson/Online Transport Archive*)

Two views on the former GCR south of the Welsh border. In the first, taken in about 1980, a southbound DMU, unusually incorporating a Swindon-built driving motor, is about to cross Hawarden Bridge (1889) which can be glimpsed in the background. The semaphore has since been replaced by coloured light signals. Three miles south is Hawarden station, located at the summit of a steep grade up from the river where ex-GWR '57xx' class 0-6-0 Pannier tank No 4683 is seen on 7 June 1965 working an unusual Whit Monday diagram described in the Supplement to the Working Timetable as 'diesel made steam'. Between 1960 and 1965, these services between Wrexham and New Brighton ran a couple of days each year when the line's DMUs were diverted elsewhere. As a result, several rakes of non-corridor carriages were retained specially for the purpose whilst the motive power was provided by Croes Newydd shed on the outskirts of Wrexham. Loadings were quite heavy as the line served several popular destinations. Built at Swindon, 4683 was in traffic from November 1944 to October 1965. The iron footbridge in the background still survives. (*Charles Roberts/Online Transport Archive; Martin Jenkins/Online Transport Archive*)

After another stiff climb including sections of 1-in-53, southbound trains arrived at Buckley Junction which opened in 1890 when the GCR created a more direct route to Wrexham. In the 1960s, cost-cutting exercises affected many stations on the Bidston-Wrexham line. In May 1964 most goods yards were closed and then in April 1969 the majority became unstaffed. By time this view was taken on 7 June 1965, trains no longer stopped here on Sundays. Because of the severe gradients, the DMUs assigned to this line usually had two power cars. (*Martin Jenkins/Online Transport Archive*)

A mile and half south of Buckley is Penyffordd for Leeswood (now abbreviated to Penyffordd) which opened in 1877. Although closed in May 1964, the goods yard reopened for a time as a coal distribution centre. This view is taken from the north end of the station on 7 June 1965 and shows 75010 bringing a mixed freight off the curve connecting with the former L&NWR Chester-Denbigh line which remained open for freight as far as Rhydymwyn until 1978. A signalbox, which replaced the one seen here in 1972, is still in place and controls movements in and out of Padeswood cement works some distance to the north. 75010 was in traffic from November 1951 to October 1967. (*Martin Jenkins/Online Transport Archive*)

Over the years, Crosville ran a number of routes between Chester and Wrexham, the most frequent being the direct 301 (later the D1) which came with the acquisition of the Western Transport company in 1933. Other less direct routes were provided as well, including the D25 seen here in Penyffordd which, in this late 1970s view, it is being operated by ERG271, one of Crosville's final batch of Bristol RELLs with the bus bodyshell, dating from 1973. Although fitted with well-upholstered seats to allow them to be used on express services – hence the E-prefix to the fleet number – they were delivered rather incongruously in all-over green, but changed to this green and white scheme on first repaint. This vehicle passed to the Welsh concern following the company's split and was used by a scout troop in the Wrexham area after being sold in 1988. (*Roland Williams/Online Transport Archive*)

Some industrial premises in North Wales retained withdrawn rolling stock for many years. For example, this Motor Rail (Simplex) four-wheel loco, new to Llay Hall colliery and brickworks in 1932, served at the colliery until 1949, the brickworks until 1954 and finally at Llay Main workshops after which it was dumped until scrapped in 1970. It is seen here on 4 July 1965. The Llay colliery, brickworks and main workshop were all rail connected to the Bidston-Wrexham line. (*John Ryan*)

A detour now to the L&NWR Chester-Denbigh line, which passed under the former GCR just north of Penyffordd. A short distance east was Kinnerton station, an isolated spot just yards from the English/Welsh border. The station opened in 1891 and derived much of its revenue from the transhipment of livestock, agricultural produce and machinery until the goods yard closed in 1955. Here, 75054 arrives with the 3.35pm from Chester General on 24 April 1962. Following withdrawal of the passenger service a few days later, the line was retained and some workmen's trains continued running to and from Chester and Broughton & Bretton for those employed at a nearby aircraft factory until 2 September 1963. The Mold Junction to Hope Junction section was singled and survived until 1970. (John Ryan)

Mold was an important Crosville hub. It was the confluence of services from places such as Rhyl, Denbigh, Wrexham and Chester as well as three routes from Birkenhead, including the F10 seen here heading for the small village of Pantymwyn, some four miles beyond Mold, The vehicle is SNL871, one of 364 Leyland Nationals delivered new between 1972 and 1983. SNL871 passed to Crosville Wales when the company was split, for whom it ran for two years before being sold. It had a further two years running in the independent sector. On 18 August 1982, the bus has just passed over the railway bridge by the site of the former Mold station. Operations at the time were managed by an inspector based in the building on the right but a bus station was opened nearby in the early 1990s. (Jonathan Cadwallader)

A delightful, late Autumn scene on the Chester-Denbigh line as Standard Class 4 75028 speeds towards Rhydymwyn with the 9.30am Ruthin to Chester on 18 November 1961. Since the end of the Second World War, passenger loadings had dropped dramatically so two carriages usually sufficed. The line was double track throughout and latterly there were some eight trains a day in each direction. This loco will be seen later working on the former Cambrian Railway (page 89). (John Ryan)

About halfway between Rhydymwyn and Denbigh is Caerwys. Here an unidentified Standard Class 4 pulls into the deserted station with the 3pm Ruthin to Chester on 25 April 1962. Although located about a mile from the village, this had been one of the busiest stations on the line with a substantial goods yard capable of handling the bulk movement of timber. Note the wheelbarrow, the porter's trolley and the wall mounted lamps. The station building, which dates from 1869, is still in existence. The line closed to all traffic just five days later on 30 April 1962. (John Ryan)

The ancient market town of Denbigh was the meeting point for the lines from Chester and Rhyl. The first station opened in 1858 but, two years later, it was replaced by a splendid Tudor Gothic-style building with a single platform. In 1862, the line was extended south to Ruthin and in 1885 the platform was extended so it could accommodate trains going in either direction. The substantial yard handled all manner of goods including livestock, agricultural produce and machinery, timber and coal. Despite dwindling passenger revenue, freight remained sufficiently profitable to justify considerable investment as late as 1957. However, a rapid slump followed. Passenger traffic ended on 30 April 1962 together with regular goods to Ruthin leaving Denbigh open until 1 March 1965. Waiting to depart for Chester General with the 12.15pm ex-Ruthin on 31 March 1962 is 42463, one of a large number of 2-6-4 tank engines designed by the LMS for suburban passenger work. The whole station site was subsequently cleared. (*Charles Firminger/Online Transport Archive*)

Although timetabled passenger services over the 12 mile section from Corwen East to Ruthin had been withdrawn in February 1953, the single track line was still used until the end of the 1961 summer season by the Radio Cruises described on page 36. The 'North Wales Radio Land Cruise' travelled anti-clockwise, starting at Pwllheli at 10.10am – attracting patrons from the Butlin's Holiday Camp at Penychain – and finishing at Criccieth at 5.14pm, from where road connections were provided. These circular tours were well patronised and offered participants 'an individual armchair seat, facilities for light meals and refreshments plus a descriptive 'radio' commentary over a loudspeaker system. Here, 75026 passes the former Eyarth station (1864) on 23 August 1961 as it heads north towards Denbigh and the coast. This 150 mile scenic cruise (cost £1) ran for the last time on 8 September 1961. Eyarth retained freight facilities until 1962 and the line remained intact until 1965. The station building is now a guest house. (*John Ryan*)

Returning to the Wrexham area with a view on the former GWR line from Chester which opened in 1846. Here, 45000 pounds through Rossett on its 42-mile non-stop dash from Chester to Shrewsbury on 27 May 1966. These '60mph expresses' continued until the Birkenhead Woodside-London Paddington services ended in March 1967. Although Rossett station had closed in October 1964, it catered for occasional 'specials' serving a nearby girls' school for some years afterwards. The signal box (right) had replaced an older structure in 1960. From here, the signalman controlled the level crossing as well as access to the goods yard which remained open until October 1968. Over the years, its sidings handled coal, coke, livestock, general goods and parcels. Reflecting the line's reduced status, most of the route was singled in the 1980s, although the section north from Rossett has since been redoubled. 45000 was the first of the 842 'Black Fives' to be built, emerging from Crewe Works early in 1935, and was officially preserved after its withdrawal in October 1967. (*Martin Jenkins/Online Transport Archive*)

Two contrasting views of Gresford. The first features Gresford Bank, a major challenge for engine crews on the '60mph expresses' with its daunting four-mile ascent at a maximum grade of 1-in-82. Problems sometimes occurred when slower moving goods traffic clogged the line. Also, by the time this 'Black Five' was tackling the grade on 30 April 1966, crews had to be fully alert as many engines were suffering the effects of reduced maintenance. In the second view, *The Welshman,* an 0-6-0 saddle tank built by Manning Wardle in 1890, is at work within Gresford Colliery. Opened as late as 1911 this was one of the deepest mines in Denbighshire. It had a relatively short life closing in July 1973 as coal reserves were exhausted and major geological problems discovered. Today its pithead gear is preserved as a memorial to the 266 men who lost their lives in September 1934 due to an underground explosion. *The Welshman,* which was new to nearby Llay Main colliery, moved to Gresford in 1965. By 1971 it was stored in Nottinghamshire as part of the NCB's official collection and, after a rather nomadic existence, now awaits restoration at the Foxfield Railway. (*John Ryan; Nigel Bowker*)

Some five miles due west of Gresford is Brymbo, in part of a dense network of lines serving local mines, quarries and steelworks. In the first view taken on 31 May 1968, a Stanier 8F 2-8-0 is seen with a rake of empties on the double track at Broughton Crossing. Visible on the skyline is the massive Brymbo Steelworks which was first established at the end of the eighteenth century. In the 1930s it produced, among other things, engineering steel for Rolls Royce aero engines. In 1948 it became part of GKN and subsequently benefited from periodic expansion until the early 1970s. However, faced by competition from cheaper imports, the works finally closed in 1990 with a loss of 1,000 jobs, rail connection having ended in 1982. Nearly all short haul mineral duties in this area were worked by locos from nearby Croes Newydd shed which also provided the motive power for the Stephenson Locomotive Society (SLS) 'Wrexham & District Rail Tour' held on 18 April 1959. Among the photo stops was one at Brymbo station (1882) used by both GWR and LMS passenger services. Although the former was abandoned in 1931, an 8½ mile service from Mold continued until March 1950 by which time there were just two weekday trains in each direction mainly for school children. Freight traffic ended in November 1964 although trains to and from the steelworks passed through for many more years. 1660 and 1635 were from a class of 0-6-0 Hawksworth Pannier tanks built between 1949 and 1955. 1635 was withdrawn after just eight years in October 1959 and 1666 after eleven years in February 1966. (*John Ryan; Charles Firminger/Online Transport Archive*)

The climb up to the steelworks was steep with the heaviest trains often needing a banking engine. On the ascent, locos usually worked chimney first and bunker or tender first going down. In the first view taken in July 1965, 6665 storms up the sweeping S-bend on the approach to Middle Brymbo with 6651 assisting at the rear. Popular with enginemen, these powerful 0-6-2Ts were versatile and reliable and had good acceleration having been designed for heavy coal trains in the south of Wales. Built by Armstrong Whitworth in 1928, these two lasted just three more months. On cresting the grade, the loaded coal wagons were pushed onto the exchange sidings where they were uncoupled and taken forward by the steelworks' own locos. Beyond Middle Brymbo, the line, now single track, climbed through attractive scenery to Minera Lime Works. In the second view, 43088 slowly descends the grade between Mount Sion and Brymbo West level crossings with a rake of loaded lime hoppers on 24 April 1967. This was from a class of 162 Ivatt 2-6-0s built for mixed traffic duties between 1947 and 1952. This one, which had emerged from Doncaster works in late 1950, was only in steam for eight more months. (*Martin Jenkins/Online Transport Archive; Richard Thompson/Online Transport Archive*)

For quite some time, Pannier tank 9610 was one of the 'regulars' on the Minera line. However, when this view was taken in September 1966 its demise was imminent. Although shorn of cabside and genuine smoke-box number plates, it was reasonably clean because, together with 9630, it had been spruced up in order to operate 'The Holyhead & Brymbo Special' on 21 August. Here, it takes water at the site of Coed Poeth station which had opened in 1897 when the GWR introduced a passenger service. After this was discontinued in 1931, most of the single platform stations were demolished although the water column, yard office, signal box and level crossing survived here. After July 1954, it was the only manned crossing to remain. (*John Strange/Graham Jackson collection*)

Still with 9610, which in the first view is leaving the exchange sidings close to the Minera Lime Works on one of its last ever duties. The Works enjoyed something of a see-saw existence; for example, in 1933 it closed due to the Great Depression coupled with a crippling coal strike and did not reopen until 1954 when there was increased demand for lime for road building. The Works closed for good in 1972, a year after rail activity came to an end, although quarrying continued until 1993. Focus of the second view is *Olwen* the Lime Works internal loco which was conveniently posed when the SLS 'Wrexham & District Rail Tour' visited the site on 18 April 1959. Looking smart in its green livery with red trim, it was built by Beyer Peacock in 1910 but was replaced in 1963 by a Ruston & Hornsby diesel shunter. Note the different height buffers. For some time, the Works also had a narrow gauge internal line using petrol and diesel shunters. *(John Strange/Graham Jackson collection; Charles Firminger/Online Transport Archive)*

The bustling market town of Wrexham is a major bus and rail hub. It is also at the centre of the largest conurbation in North Wales. In times past, it was served by a plethora of independent bus operators running in parallel with the all-powerful Crosville. One such was E Wright & Son, who were based in the village of Penycae near Ruabon, initially running a twice a week service to and from Wrexham. From formation in 1924, the business was unusual in buying new rather than second-hand vehicles, including this 41-seat Burlingham-bodied Commer Avenger IV in 1959. Seen on 9 September 1967 with a decent load of passengers, it is about to pull into its allocated bay at Wrexham's substantial bus station. Wright's took advantage of bus deregulation in 1986 by significantly enlarging its fleet and registering a number of services in direct competition with Crosville Wales. However, this proved to be unsustainable and the company ceased trading in 1993. (*R.L. Wilson/Online Transport Archive*)

Crosville's expansion through acquisition brought with it companies of all sizes, right down to some single vehicle operators. At the other end of the scale were substantial businesses such as Western Transport of Wrexham acquired in 1933, whose fleet of 133 vehicles made Crosville the dominant operator in the town. By 1954 the large depot on Mold Road housed 125 operational buses, about 10% of the company's entire fleet, and there was still sufficient room for a dumping ground for all manner of elderly withdrawn vehicles which acted as a magnet for visiting enthusiasts. The sheer number of services operated from the depot meant that when the area-based system of route numbers was adopted in 1959, those in Wrexham were allocated numbers in three series: D, E (local services) and G (workpeople's and school services). Photographs of the E routes are not common, but here a 1949 ECW-bodied, AEC-engined Bristol K DKA331 is seen in High Street on the E2. With a running time of only 10-12 minutes between Hightown and General railway station, the crew have seemingly taken advantage of the two destinations being adjacent on the blind and have set it in 'lazy' style to avoid having to keep changing it. The bus was scrapped when withdrawn in 1966. (*Jack Barlow/Online Transport Archive*)

The history of Wrexham's three stations is quite complex. Two adjacent sites were developed by the Wrexham, Mold and Connah's Quay Railway (seen here, opened 1866) and the GWR (to the right, 1846). The former gained the suffix Exchange when the line was extended the short distance to Wrexham Central in 1887, whilst the GWR station became Wrexham General in BR days. This view illustrates the effects of the Beeching cuts when stations were closed or reduced in status, tracks lifted and platforms and buildings left to crumble whilst attempts were also made to improve reliability by the introduction of DMUs, even on lines that were under threat. Vehement local opposition prevented closure of the former GCR line to Bidston but couldn't stop abandonment of the well-used service to Chester Northgate which succumbed in September 1968. Subsequently, Exchange became an unstaffed halt in April 1969, fought off another closure attempt in 1970 and was reduced to single track status in 1973. Here, a two-car Derby-built DMU is seen on 27 January 1978, the building on the left being subsequently demolished. The name finally ceased to exist in June 1981 when Exchange was absorbed into General. (*David Ventry*)

Located close to the town centre Wrexham Central (1887) was later rebuilt with five platform faces, single storey wooden buildings and a footbridge connecting the through lines in order to accommodate the extra traffic generated by the opening of a 12¼ mile branch to Ellesmere in 1895. In the background is St Giles Church, whose pinnacled tower is one of 'Seven Wonders of Wales'. Here, 1458 waits to leave with the 1.30pm two carriage auto-train to Ellesmere. The 0-4-2 tank engine is from a class of 75 motor-fitted locos built between 1932 and 1936 for push-pull operation on lightly loaded lines. Latterly, the Ellesmere branch, which last ran on 8 September 1962, had eight weekday return workings usually worked by auto trains. The goods yard at Wrexham Central closed in December 1964 and the station then became unstaffed. The line from Exchange was reduced to a single track stub in August 1973 when all remaining buildings were demolished. Central was moved to a new site ¼ mile back towards Exchange/General in 1998 to allow for the construction of shops and a car park. (*Photographer unknown/Graham Jackson collection*)

Only three stations on the single track line to Ellesmere had passing loops, one of which was at Marchwiel. When an ordnance factory was established here during the Second World War, the volume of traffic led to suspension of the uneconomic passenger service between 1940 and 1946. In the first view the single line token is about to be handed over as 1458 is recorded on a frosty day shortly before the end of passenger services. Following closure of the passenger service, the line was retained as far as Pickhill Halt, just south of Marchwiel, to provide access to a Cadbury's factory seen in the background of the second view taken on 21 February 1967. Filthy 75021 from Croes Newydd shed has arrived with a rake of empty vans and will soon reverse onto the siding into the factory. This Cadbury's traffic ended in December 1971 after which the line remained open to Marchwiel until May 1973 and finally as far as Abenbury for occasional deliveries of china clay until May 1981. (*E.C. Bennett & Martin Jenkins/Online Transport Archive; E.J. McWatt/Online Transport Archive*)

The opening of a major Royal Ordnance Factory north of Marchweil during the Second World War created a massive demand for workpeople's transport and this continued after the war as the site was converted for civilian use. At shift change time, convoys of buses, frequently some of the oldest in the Crosville fleet, ferried people to and from their home villages or into Wrexham town centre. In March 1968, DKB380, a Bristol K6B with ECW lowbridge bodywork, is seen leaving the estate. Between 1946 and 1953, Crosville took delivery of 279 Bristol Ks and the later KSW variant to add to 22 war-time Utility examples and a batch of 14 from London Transport, with disposals taking place between 1959 and 1968. *(Alan Mortimer/Online Transport Archive)*

By far the busiest station on the Ellesmere branch was Overton-on-Dee which had a long passing loop, goods shed, crane and yard with livestock pens. Nearby was a brick works and dairy, the latter being converted to produce munitions during the war. The station was also used to transfer wounded soldiers to a military hospital at Penley. In this view, the branch 'regular' 1458 is pushing its single auto-carriage towards Wrexham on 21 July 1962. The 0-4-2 tanks used on this line were based at Oswestry. *(John Ryan)*

South-west of Wrexham is Rhos – Rhosllanerchrugog to give it its full name – which was first accessed by rail from the south in 1867 and then by a GWR branch from Rhos Junction on the Wrexham-Shrewsbury line in 1901, when this single platform station was built. Note the elevated iron water tank, passing loop, signal box and siding into the brickworks dominating the background. Although regular passenger traffic ended in 1931, specials were run for the 1945 Eisteddfod and for Wrexham FC home matches until the signal box closed in 1952. When the SLS 'Wrexham & District Rail Tour' visited on 18 April 1959, Panniers 1635 and 1660 were in charge of the last passenger-carrying train to stop here. Goods traffic finally ended on 14 October 1963. (*Charles Firminger/Online Transport Archive*)

After the decline of the of the mining industry in the Wrexham area, demand for workpeople's transport reduced significantly but buses still provided a vital lifeline for communities on the outskirts of the urban area. In this December 1979 view, passengers board the D11 (Minera-Wrexham) in the former mining village of Coedpoeth. Although SRG225 is another ubiquitous Bristol RE, it is unusual because it has Marshall bodywork, being one of 123 vehicles taken into the Crosville fleet in 1972 from the North Western Road Car Company when it was split by the National Bus Company (NBC) between neighbouring operators. Most remained at former North Western depots in Northwich, Macclesfield and Biddulph, but a small number migrated to Welsh depots towards the end of their lives. Mold Road depot in Wrexham was closed by Crosville Wales in 1991 and the site sold for housing. (*Roland Williams/ Online Transport Archive*)

In its final days, Croes Newydd shed (1902), which lay to the west of Wrexham town centre, was a magnet for photographers as it housed some of the last former GWR type locos still in operation. Until 31 December 1962, it had been a BR Western Region outpost but then everything changed when control passed to the London Midland Region and the shed code changed from 84J to 6C. Furthermore, the LM authorities drafted in other locos to replace GWR types although some of these survived, often in very poor condition, almost until the shed closed in June 1967. Any unofficial visit to a loco shed was always a little hit or miss. Some shed foremen were easy-going – 'take care and mind the pits' – others simply refused entry at which point 'other ways' could sometimes be found to enter the inner sanctum. On 27 May 1966, 6C still had some 30 engines for its remaining freight diagrams. In the foreground is 48325, whilst 6697 and 48252 are on the coaling stage line. The two 8Fs were built during the war and survived until May 1968. 6697 of 1928 was withdrawn just days later but is now preserved. (*Martin Jenkins/Online Transport Archive*)

The shed was located in the middle of a triangle of tracks. Looking towards Shrewsbury, the marshalling yard at Watery Lane was quite busy on 29 August 1972 as Brush Type 4 1710 transports ingots destined for Shotton Steelworks along the main line. This locomotive had entered traffic in early 1964 and, after being renumbered 47121, remained in service until 1996. Shunting in the yard is 5039 which was built at Crewe in 1959 and withdrawn in 1976. (*Barry Shore*)

With exchange sidings adjacent to the Wrexham-Ruabon mainline, in 1986 Bersham colliery was the last Denbighshire coalfield to close, due to unfavourable economic conditions and falling markets. In the past it had supplied places such as Brymbo and Shotton Steelworks and the power station at Fiddler's Ferry. Opened in 1864, it was subsequently upgraded several times after the Second World War. Steam reigned supreme until arrival of the first diesel in 1980, the tight curvature of the internal track layout dictating the use of 0-4-0 locos. The first view is of the long-serving *Shakespeare*, built in 1914 by R & W Hawthorn, Leslie, which came to the colliery in about 1928 and stayed until being scrapped in 1980. The second view. taken on 27 August 1976, shows *Hornet* shunting wagons at the coal-loading screens. This saddle tank was built by Peckett in 1937 and came to Bersham from Ifton Colliery. Today it is preserved at the Ribble Steam Railway at Preston. (*Nigel Bowker; John Ryan*)

In 1862, 16 years after the opening of the mainline, the remodelled station at Ruabon became a junction for services to Bala and Barmouth complete with goods depot, marshalling yard and turntable. In the first view taken on 18 June 1963, 'Jubilee' 4-6-0 *Galatea* prepares to head north towards Wrexham. Built at Crewe in 1936 it was withdrawn in the November but escaped the scrapman and is now preserved, regularly hauling railtours in the north of England. Once employing 60 men, facilities at Ruabon were slowly reduced until it became unstaffed by 1974. A short distance to the south was Wynnstay Colliery (1856-1927) the remains of which can be seen to the right of 92021 as it steams towards Shrewsbury with a lengthy train of vans on 4 March 1967. This loco is of particular interest as it was one of ten BR Standard Class 9F 2-10-0s built at Crewe in 1955 with Franco-Crosti boilers. When these locos were later rebuilt along more conventional lines they were classified as 8F due to their smaller boilers and could be distinguished by their lack of front smoke deflectors. This one remained active for another eight months. This area was riddled with branches feeding into nearby brickworks, collieries, iron and limestone works and this view was taken from the bridge abutments of a former mineral line leading from the colliery. *(Fred Ivey; Martin Jenkins/Online Transport Archive)*

North and Mid-Wales had relatively little by way of inland navigation. The late eighteenth century saw ambitious plans for canals connecting the Dee, Mersey and Severn Rivers via the lucrative North East Wales coalfields, but only a small proportion was built. A branch westwards from the Shropshire Union Canal at Hurleston near Nantwich to Llangollen, which required the construction of several imposing structures, was opened in 1805. Although initially successful, a sharp fall in traffic after the First World War led to its abandonment for navigation in 1944, although it was retained intact to ensure a supply of water to the Shropshire Union main line. Signs of dereliction are clear in this 1961 image of the Trevor Basin, west of Ruabon, where there had been exchange sidings linked to local industry. By this time, the growing leisure market was already beginning to have an impact and this site is today a thriving marina for narrow boats. Adjacent is one of the most remarkable engineering structures in North Wales. Designed by Thomas Telford and Williams Jessop and opened in 1805, the Pontcysyllte aqueduct is one of the great monuments of the industrial revolution. It has 18 arches, is 127ft high, 336 yards long, 12ft wide and has a sheer drop on one side with only a narrow footpath and parapet on the other. It has been known for the faint-hearted to lie on the bottom of boats as they cross over. This view taken on 11 October 1969 shows two hire boats edging their way across, the one in the rear being the *Connah*. An 11 mile stretch of the canal, including the aqueducts at Pontcysyllte and Chirk, was recognised as a UNESCO World Heritage site in 2009. (J.G. Parkinson/Online Transport Archive; John Pigott)

Just over six miles west of Ruabon is Llangollen, the first major stop on the 54-mile line to Barmouth, other sections of which will be seen on pages 108-115. This is one of the most popular towns in North Wales visited by thousands each year, many of whom come for the annual International Eisteddfod. During the season, many excursions were run from Birmingham and the Midlands and scheduled trains were always well-used. The station is on quite a curve and hugs the north bank of the river. In this view, 4-6-0 7801 *Anthony Manor* assisted by 2-6-0 'Mogul' 7314 are heading towards Barmouth on 29 September 1962 with a Talyllyn Railway Preservation Society AGM special whilst another 'Mogul', 6301, waits to receive the token to proceed east along the single track towards Ruabon. The decision to abandon this important cross-country line provoked considerable local anger. Closure was set for 16 January 1965 but nature intervened when flooding severed the line at Carrog on the night of 11/12 December 1964. Temporary services were introduced on either side until these were discontinued on 16 January. Goods traffic continued between Ruabon and Llangollen until the end of March 1968. Since 1975, the Llangollen Railway has operated a heritage service which now extends to the outskirts of Corwen and has thankfully survived severe financial problems in early 2021. All three locos were built at Swindon: 6301 in 1920, withdrawn October 1962; 7314 in 1921, withdrawn February 1963; and 7801 in 1938, withdrawn July 1965. (*Derek J. Lowe Archive*)

Crosville was a late convert to the concept of rear-engined, one-man operated double deckers. Although sister companies in the BTC and then NBC had been taking delivery of the Bristol VR since 1969, Crosville's first examples did not arrive until 1975, with Welsh depots not seeing their first examples until 1978. By the time this picture was taken, Crosville had just received the last of its 243 VRs, although ironically the company was to go on to accumulate many older, second-hand examples. Wrexham-based DVG528, a Gardner-engined Series 3 example, with 74-seat ECW body, is seen in Llangollen awaiting departure on the 25 mile trunk D1 to Chester. The 'Wrexham' fleetname dates from a few months previously when the NBC's Market Analysis Project (MAP) resulted in the reorganisation of services under local marketing names. DVG528 passed to Crosville Wales on the split of the company in 1986. (*Roland Williams/Online Transport Archive*)

Returning to the mainline, Chirk Viaduct provides an impressive backdrop for this view of one of the last '60mph expresses' hauled by 45052. Built by Vulcan Foundry in 1934, this 'Black Five' was withdrawn in September 1967. Fortunately, trains still cross the viaduct which dates from 1848. Rebuilt ten years later, it is 849ft long and consists of 16 arches of which ten form the main span rising 100ft above the River Ceiriog. Alongside is Chirk Aqueduct on the Llangollen Branch of the canal. (*Gavin Morrison*)

Gobowen was once a busy junction on the Wrexham-Shrewsbury line from which a branch to Oswestry was opened in 1848. In this view, taken on 18 June 1963, a northbound express is headed by 'Jubilee' class 45660 *Rooke,* which emerged from Derby Works in 1934 and was withdrawn in June 1966. Many of the period features of the station remain in situ today, with the main building (right) now being Grade II listed. (*Fred Ivey*)

The ancient market town of Oswestry was first reached by the GWR from Gobowen in 1848. Its transformation into a major railway town followed completion of the Whitchurch to Welshpool line in 1864, when many historic buildings were demolished in order to build the substantial Cambrian Railways (CR) station which also served as the company's headquarters as seen on the left. Also constructed were workshop facilities, carriage and wagon sidings, loco shed, turntable, goods shed and cattle pens. In 1924, the original GWR station closed, and a bay platform was added to the CR station for use by the Gobowen shuttle. Although once served by through passenger trains from London Euston to Aberystwyth via Crewe, the CR route to Welshpool was never as important as that from Shrewsbury. Despite heavy use during the Second World War, traffic declined during the 1950s and the Whitchurch-Welshpool line was listed for closure in the Beeching Report. As a result, passenger services ended on 16 January 1965 leaving just the branch from Gobowen. The loco shed closed in 1965 and goods traffic ended in 1971. Seen in the first view at the head of a permanent way train is 46513, one of a small group of BR Ivatt Class 2 2-6-0s built at Swindon during 1952/53. These sturdy, versatile engines were specially designed for stopping passenger and mixed-traffic duties and were quite at home ambling between stations or hauling expresses at 60mph. Their capacious cabs also made them popular with crews. In the second view, BR Hawksworth 0-6-0 Pannier tank 1638 sweeps round the curve at the south end of the station with a ballast train. Both scenes date from August 1963. (*Derek Penney (both)*)

During the latter days of steam, Croes Newydd based 1638 was a regular on the Tanat Valley line which had opened in full by 1904. Although built to serve local mines and quarries and carry livestock and agricultural produce, traffic was never heavy. Competition from road transport saw a fall from a peak of 145,000 tons in 1930 to just over 1000 tons in 1951, the year before the line closed to passengers. In the first view, 1638 is pictured at the limit of the line at Llangynog on 4 January 1964 on what was probably the last ever working along the full line. Following its withdrawal in August 1966, 1638 is the only BR 'low bridge' Pannier to survive into preservation. Later in 1964, an unidentified Ivatt 2-6-0 heads a ballast train across the A495 by the former Porth-y-waen Halt. The line from Gobowen, through Oswestry to the Tanat Valley quarries, continued in use for aggregates traffic after the cessation of the Oswestry passenger shuttle in 1966. It closed officially in 1992, with the last freights having run a couple of years earlier, although plans for a heritage passenger service are well-advanced. A separate heritage railway scheme exists at Nantmawr. (John Ryan; John Collingwood/Online Transport Archive)

The 8½ mile branch from Llanymynech to Llanfyllin opened in 1863 and, except for a very busy spell during construction of Lake Vyrnwy Reservoir in the 1880s, it led an uneventful life. Latterly, trains carried few passengers with just four weekday return workings supplemented by an extra diagram on Saturday evenings. For some time, traffic had been in the hands of Ivatt 2MT 2-6-0s, one of which is seen in the first view at Llanfyllin, two carriages being more than sufficient. Problems occurred on the last night, Saturday 16 January 1965, as the last scheduled working was booked to return as empty stock to Oswestry. At first, the guard refused to let the 100 or so people back on board. It had passed 10pm and everything was pitch black. Finally, he reluctantly relented and allowed everyone to return to Llanymynech. During the mass closures of the Beeching era, most railway employees remained friendly towards responsible enthusiasts but others, clearly angered by the run-down, could be openly hostile. Curiously, Llanymynech station is in England but part of the main A483 road through the village is the actual border with Wales. Close to areas rich in mineral deposits, it soon developed into a significant junction with four platforms, station buffet and goods yard. To handle the volume of traffic the CR also doubled the line north to Oswestry. In the second view, taken on 18 June 1963, 46515 has just arrived from Llanfyllin. To its right are the one time tracks of the grandly named but short-lived Potteries, Shrewsbury and North Wales Railway. Known as the 'Pots' it was opened between Shrewsbury and Llanymynech in 1866 but had closed by 1880. It was then re-opened in 1911 by the Shropshire & Montgomeryshire (S&M) but led a very precarious existence until taken over by the military to transport ammunition during the Second World War. This line closed in 1960, followed in July 1964 by Llanymynech goods yard and those on the Llanfyllin branch and finally everything south of Llynclys on 16 January 1965. (*Gavin Morrison; Fred Ivey*)

In 1871, the S&M opened a branch to Criggion to serve a stone quarry, this traffic lasting until 1933. During the war when the line was taken over by the Ministry of Defence, stone traffic resumed but the S&M was always on a financial knife-edge. Knowing the network was under threat, the SLS organised a tour on 28 September 1958 when members were transported along the branch sitting inside a coupled pair of MOD Drewry railcars. The first view is at the border village of Melverley, whose residents crossed the River Severn into Wales by walking over the railway bridge. The second scene at Criggion shows both railcars including WD No 9105, whilst lurking in the shed is the quarry company's 1927 Sentinel BE class, four-wheel, vertical-boilered, locomotive which had hauled freight trains along the line but was by now relegated to local shunting duties. When the MOD pulled out the following year, stone traffic ceased again and the remnants of the S&M closed in February 1960. (R.W.A. Jones/Online Transport Archive; John McCann/Online Transport Archive)

A few miles south-west from Criggion is Pool Quay on the former CR main line from Oswestry. Opened in 1860, it was upgraded in 1896 when a passing loop was installed. In the first view, the signalman is ready to hand the single track token to the fireman of BR Standard Class 4 80080 as it approaches with the 12.06 from Welshpool to Whitchurch on 2 January 1965. The goods yard had closed in May 1964 and this section south from Llynclys was last used on 16 January 1965. Built at Brighton in 1951, this loco was preserved after it was withdrawn in July 1965. The second view is at Buttington Junction where the CR joined the former joint GWR and L&NWR line from Shrewsbury. The station here closed before the Beeching cuts at the end of the 1960 summer season. 7800 *Torquay Manor* is heading a southbound train in August 1964, the month in which the loco was withdrawn. It is from a pre-war batch of 20 'Manors' built at Swindon. (*John Ryan; Vincent Ventry, courtesy David Ventry*)

Immediately prior to the Second World War, North and Mid-Wales was still home to a wonderful variety of narrow gauge railways. After the war, prospects did not look good but there was a growing belief amongst railway enthusiasts that they should be preserved and operated as seasonal attractions for visitors. From the early 1970s, the survivors have been marketed under the banner The Great Little Trains of Wales. One of these is the Welshpool and Llanfair Light Railway (W&L). Owned originally by the CR, this 2ft 6in gauge line, which connected the main line at Welshpool to Llanfair Caereinion, did not actually open until 1903, although proposals had existed since 1864. Unfortunately, the line never generated the expected traffic, so passenger services were abandoned in 1931, by which time ownership had passed to the GWR, but freight operations continued until November 1956 under BR control. Traffic from Llanfair consisted mainly of livestock and agricultural produce with household coal in the reverse direction. 823 is shunting in the yard in Welshpool in July 1954. The locomotive was one of two 0-6-0Ts built by Beyer, Peacock for the opening of the line. Originally named *The Earl* (No 1) and *The Countess* (No 2), they later became GWR/BR 822 and 823, but, by this time, they no longer carried names. (*John McCann/Online Transport Archive*)

From Welshpool station, the line passed through the centre of town, partly on street and partly on private right of way between rows of terraced houses. *The Countess* is seen on the edge of town in the middle of a busy junction at Raven Square just before entering the alignment through to Llanfair. The absence of number plates indicates the view was taken after the line had passed to preservationists. Sadly, the town council would not permit the continued operation of the street section, so this was abandoned after a small number of enthusiast events in the early 1960s. Much of the town section can still be traced on foot with the help of a series of informative display boards. (*Phil Tatt/ Online Transport Archive*)

The preservation group made steady progress reinstating a tourist service from their base at Llanfair Caereinion to Castle Caereinion in 1963, Sylfaen in 1972, and Raven Square in 1981, where a substantial terminal station was built. Both of the original locomotives have been available for much of the intervening time but supplemented by engines acquired or loaned from other 2ft 6in (760mm) lines from around the world. Sadly, the original coaching stock was scrapped in the 1930s, but notable replacements came from the Zillertalbahn in Austria and from Sierra Leone. The line is blessed with attractive scenery and substantial structures at river and valley crossings. Here No 5, *Nutty*, a 1924 four-wheel, vertical boiler Sentinel, heads a work train over Brynelin Viaduct in March 1967. Having previously worked at Fletton Brickworks near Peterborough, *Nutty* reached the W&L in 1964 but is now at the Leighton Buzzard Narrow Gauge Railway. (*Phil Tatt/Online Transport Archive*)

Straddling the Wales/England border, Mid-Wales Motorways has been through a number of incarnations but has always remained a draw for the enthusiast because of its fascinating fleet. The original company was formed in 1937 by the amalgamation of six small independents, and a further 12 were absorbed in the period up to 1951. Because of financial difficulty, the company was liquidated in September 1963, but a 'phoenix' business – Mid-Wales Motorways (1963) Limited – was formed almost immediately. A disastrous depot fire in 1969 caused further difficulty, but the company survived until 1991 in various forms and even today still exists as Mid-Wales Travel, the trading name of Evans of Penrhyncoch, near Aberystwyth, geographically separated from its original heartland. The company's main base for much of this time was 'The Horse Repository' in Newtown, but a number of

outstations were used including Welshpool, shown here in June 1962. The vehicles are typically Mid-Wales: ex-Bristol Omnibus Duple-bodied Bedford OB MHU52 (new 1950, acquired 1959); EP9502, a Duple-bodied Guy Arab III which was new to Mid-Wales in 1947; and CEP147, a 1951 Sentinel STC4 integral, also new to Mid-Wales. The Sentinel was destroyed in the depot fire, the Guy was scrapped in 1963 but the Bedford survives in preservation. *(Phil Tatt/Online Transport Archive)*

Crosville Bristol LD6B DLB732 is rather dwarfed by the imposing edifice of Welshpool station. It was designed by Benjamin Piercy in the French Gothic style for the opening of the Oswestry-Abermule section of the Oswestry & Newtown Railway, whose headquarters were housed within the building, in 1860. Both the building and the railway survive today – the latter forming part of the Cambrian mainline between Shrewsbury and Aberystwyth – but incongruously are now separated from each other by a road. The original railway alignment was absorbed by the Welshpool bypass in 1991/92, with its new formation taking the line slightly to the east where just a basic platform and shelter is provided. The former station has Grade II Listed Building status, so was thankfully retained when its adjacent platforms were removed, and now houses a series of retail outlets. The bus is on route D71, which provided an hourly Welshpool-Guilsfield-Oswestry service. It was in the Crosville fleet from 1955 to 1970 after which it was employed by the Castrol oil company at their plant in Ellesmere Port until scrapped in 1976. *(Marcus Eavis/Online Transport Archive)*

Following the opening of its station in 1860, the ancient market town of Welshpool eventually became a major junction with goods trains passing through or being assembled in the station sidings. There were also servicing facilities for locomotives only working this far. For example, 7818 *Granville Manor* had arrived on a stopping train from Aberystwyth and was replaced for the onward journey by an ex-LMS tank engine. First appearing on the CR in the early 1950s, these Collett designed 'Manors' were the largest locos permitted on the Cambrian due to the line's restricted axle-load. They proved popular with engine men although some critics claimed they 'destroyed' the track. In the background, ex-GWR 0-6-0 No 2204 departs from the bay platform with the 10.10am all stations to Whitchurch. 7818 was in traffic from May 1949 to September 1963 and 2204 from August 1939 to December 1963. (*John Langford*)

Two views of Welshpool in transition. In the first, taken in late 1966, 75028 is in charge of the up 'Cambrian Coast Express' (CCE) to Shrewsbury and ultimately Paddington. First introduced by the GWR in 1927, this titled train was suspended during the Second World War but was reintroduced on summer Saturdays in 1947. From 1954, it ran every weekday, usually with nine carriages. On the left are two of the earlier examples of the BR-built Type 2 diesel-electric locomotives delivered between 1958 and 1967. The second view illustrates the station's reduced status; connecting places have been painted over on the sign and platforms reduced from four to two. By the end of the period covered by this book, there were seven up trains and six down, supplemented on Saturdays by an extra in each direction as well as two return workings on Sundays. The splendid station building symbolises a far more confident railway era. (*Gavin Morrison; Marcus Eavis/Online Transport Archive*)

This rare view is of 2538 the last of the famous ex-GWR Deans Goods to remain in operation. A total of 280 of these class '2301' 0-6-0 tender engines were built between 1883 and 1899. Designed for mixed traffic, they were highly successful with examples being requisitioned by the military during both wars and transferred overseas, not all returning safely. Just over 50 were taken over by BR but, by 1957, 2538 was the last survivor. Built at Swindon in August 1897 it was withdrawn in the May. Here, it is amongst the scenery of the Vale of Powys crossing the River Severn at Cil-Cewydd just south of Welshpool with a short pick-up goods on 24 September 1955. *(T.B. Owen/Colour-Rail.com)*

Starting at Caersws, locomotive crews faced eight miles of varied grades, reaching as much as 1-in-71, to attain the line's summit at Talerddig, 693ft above sea level. As a result, up and down trains sometimes had a pilot engine attached, especially during the holiday season, and would often pass and exchange tokens at Talerddig station. As it could only accommodate up to ten carriages, it sometimes became a bottleneck with up to four pilot or banking engines occupying the summit neck, the latter being used on the heavier trains. Coming east from Machynlleth, up trains faced even steeper grades for some 14 miles culminating in 2¼ miles at 1-in-52 including sharp curves. In the view on the right, 7800 *Torquay Manor* is heading east towards Welshpool as it approaches the short 120ft rock cutting, with almost vertical walls, close to the summit. This view gives some indication of the work involved in excavating the trackbed when the line opened in 1858. Could that be a lucky enthusiast on the footplate experiencing the 'ride of a lifetime'? Some engine men on the CR were very amenable during the dying days of steam as one of the authors can testify. The upper view depicts unassisted eastbound 7803 *Barcote Manor* slogging up the gradient with eight coaches. (*Gavin Morrison (both)*)

Machynlleth was the nerve centre of Cambrian coastal operations with the four mile single track section to Dovey Junction handling freight, passenger, empty stock and light engine movements to and from the former CR three road shed which had all facilities including a turntable. From here, locos were provided for the 'Main Road' to Aberystwyth and the 'Coast Road' to Pwllheli each of which had sub-sheds. Summer Saturdays were especially busy, when the lines east from Machynlleth could become over occupied with each signal box requiring 20 tokens for each direction. In 1959, the shed had an allocation of over 40 engines but numbers gradually declined until the shed closed to steam in 1966. When this view was taken 7827 *Lydham Manor* and 7801 *Anthony Manor* had been specially prepared as part of a quintet of 'Manors' involved in a Royal Train movement on 10 August 1963. (*Derek Penney*)

The section from Machynlleth to Aberystwyth was opened during 1863/64 but only Dovey Junction and Borth survived the station closures of May 1965. Today, the passing loop and up platform at the latter have gone as has the footbridge from which this photograph was taken. Fortunately, its fine double-storey station building with its splendid chimney stacks is Grade II listed. Although in private hands, one room is available to passengers as a waiting room at this unstaffed halt. On 18 January 1965, all passenger duties except for the CCE and the up and down Night Mails had been dieselised. To lure more customers onto the railway, a well-advertised summer Sunday service on both the 'Aber' and the 'Coast Road' was introduced in July 1970. Other enticements included a 'Western Region Mystery Excursion' to Barmouth. (*Richard Thompson/Online Transport Archive*)

The University town of Aberystwyth is at the south-western extremity of the former CR. The resort has a number of attractions including the narrow gauge Vale of Rheidol Railway (VoR). Also, until 1965, people could reach the resort by a long straggling line from Carmarthen. Engines off the two standard gauge routes were housed and serviced at a loco shed rebuilt in 1940 where 'Duke' class 4-4-0 No 9087 *Mercury,* still in GWR livery, is seen shortly before it was withdrawn in July 1949. It was from a class of 60 locos built between 1895 and 1899, of which 29 were withdrawn in the late 30s with some of their parts being used in construction of the 'Dukedogs'. The last 'Duke' was withdrawn in July 1951. (*T.B. Owen/Colour-Rail.com*)

At the north end of Aberystwyth promenade, a funicular cliff railway connects the lower part of town with the Constitution Hill leisure area, with a vertical ascent of 430ft at a gradient of more than 1 in 2. It was opened in 1896 and was initially very popular with visitors, although its fortunes began to decline around the Second World War. It was originally powered on the water balance system, whereby a water tank is filled whilst a car is at the top station and, under braking, descends and allows the other car to rise. It was converted to electric power in 1921 and ran until 1976, nine years after this July 1967 view, when its operation was suspended on safety grounds. It reopened in 1978 and is now run by a volunteer charity, with Grade II Listing. (*Phil Tatt/ Online Transport Archive*)

In the post-war years, Aberystwyth was a particular draw for holidaymakers from the West Midlands, with Midland Red operating a number of express services and tours. In the first scene, the company's home-built C1-type coach 3329 with 30-seat centre-entrance body is fully loaded and awaiting departure alongside the railway station, destined for Kidderminster. Behind is an S13 dual-purpose vehicle acting as a duplicate on this busy run. The drivers, dressed in their smart white coats and caps are checking their passenger lists to make sure that everything is in order. In the second view, somewhere near Devil's Bridge, passengers are clearly enjoying the Cambrian scenery on a day trip in July 1967. They are appreciating the comfort provided by this 1965 Duple (Northern)-bodied Leyland Leopard, one of a batch of 49 delivered that year with large panoramic windows and forced air ventilation. These vehicles had 47 seats, but this was reduced to 41 during holiday cruises to allow extra legroom. They were the first coaches to be delivered to the company after it made the decision to buy in from outside manufacturers, but the Midland Red type classification continued and they were known as LC7s. The advert above the windows is of particular interest being part of a BET Group campaign to oppose nationalisation. This proved unsuccessful as Midland Red became part of the newly formed National Bus Company in 1969. (*Phil Tatt/ Online Transport Archive (both)*)

After the cessation of main line steam in August 1968, the 1ft 11¾in gauge Vale of Rheidol (VoR) line was the only surviving steam on BR. For a period, its future seemed in jeopardy, with annual ridership having fallen to just 90,000. In the event, strong marketing as part of Great Little Trains, allied with some rationalisation at the Aberystwyth end, ensured its survival. Major changes in 1968 were the construction of a new terminus on the site of the former Carmarthen bay platform within the mainline station, and the abandonment of the loop. This crossed Park Avenue, went round the back of the Crosville bus depot and the football ground, and eventually ran parallel to the Cambrian Main line for a short distance some half a mile out of town. This busy 1967 scene shows No 8 *Llywelyn* about to cross Park Avenue, for which a man with a red flag emerged from the signalbox (right) to stop the traffic. Note the Midland Red coach which may have dropped passengers off to ride the line. (J.G. Parkinson/Online Transport Archive (both))

Other casualties of the rationalisation were the quaint engine shed and water tower which had been built for the opening in 1902. The line's original purpose was freight, particularly lead ore and timber, but the tourist potential was soon spotted with passenger operations to Devil's Bridge quickly following. The founding company was taken over by the CR in 1913, with ownership passing to the GWR in 1923 and BR in 1948. Various locomotives were employed in the early years, but, for many, the line will always be associated with three sturdy 2-6-2 tank engines of which No 7 *Owain Glyndŵr* and 8 *Llywelyn* were built by the GWR at Swindon in 1923. No 9 *Prince of Wales*, seen here being prepared for service outside the shed, is purportedly a rebuild of No 2 (later 1213), built for the opening by Davies & Metcalfe of Manchester and also named *Prince of Wales*. In reality, it was so heavily modified at Swindon that a 'new' loco virtually indistinguishable from its two sisters emerged in 1924. When this shed was demolished, the redundant main line steam depot was converted for use by the VoR. The area is now occupied by a car park. (*Phil Tatt/Online Transport Archive*)

In spite of the claims on the advertising hoardings, the VoR is perhaps not as well blessed with scenery as some of the other Great Little Trains, which also reduces opportunities for good lineside shots. In 1970, No 7 *Owain Glyndŵr* crosses the Rheidol River not long after the narrow gauge diverges from the mainline. At this time, the locomotives and coaching stock were unimaginatively painted in unrelieved Rail Blue, in line with the prevailing BR corporate identity. (*R.W.A. Jones/Online Transport Archive*)

On arrival at Devil's Bridge many people visit the nearby eponymous structure, which is actually three bridges superimposed on one another, for a view of the spectacular waterfall. On 20 July 1963, *Owain Glyndŵr* is seen in the earlier BR Brunswick Green livery, with the lion and wheel totem. The 11¾ mile line remained in BR ownership until 1989 when it was sold off as part of BR privatisation to a company associated with the Brecon Mountain Railway. In more recent times, line has hosted visiting locomotives and there are plans for a museum to display narrow gauge locomotives from around the world. (*John Ryan*)

Crosville's presence in Aberystwyth began with the takeover of services from Jones Brothers, who traded as Red and White Bus Services, not to be confused with the better-known company in Chepstow. From their base, Crosville developed a far-flung network of services which eventually reached as far south as Newcastle Emlyn when operating areas in NBC were changed in the early 1970s. The town was also a centre for some Crosville express services as well as occasional seasonal tours, such as this afternoon excursion to the Clywedog Dam for the princely sum of £1.25. ERG160 was a classic Bristol RELH6G with ECW 49-seat bodywork. When new in 1970, it had worked flagship express routes from Liverpool to London, or to North Wales destinations, and was classified CRG (full coach). Initially it was painted in cream and black coach livery, but soon succumbed to NBC all-over white. As with many Crosville coaches, it was downgraded for more menial work late in life, being fitted with one-man operation equipment and painted in the green and white dual-purpose livery. It was withdrawn in December 1982. (*Roland Williams/Online Transport Archive*)

Titled trains have always captured the public imagination. In August 1963, 7828 *Odney Manor,* displays a 'Cambrian Coast Express' (CCE) headboard as it passes the four road Aberystwyth loco shed prior to coupling up to the 9.45 morning departure which took an hour to reach Dovey Junction, where the Pwllheli portion would be attached for the ongoing journey to Shrewsbury and Paddington, arrival time 4pm. However, at this time, delays were frequent and students at the University often felt 'trapped' as it took so long to get anywhere by road or rail. 7828 was one of ten 'Manors' built at Swindon in 1950 and was subsequently preserved. Also on shed are 75023 and 80099. In the second view taken in the early 1970s, Class 24 5078 is at the head of the daily mail train whilst the DMU has arrived on an all stations from Shrewsbury. The long platforms had once accommodated lengthy seasonal excursions. The run round middle road is still in situ and the interchange with the VoR is on the left side. Today, the station buildings, clock tower and concourse still remain although only one platform is now required. Note the Wall's Ice Cream lorry on the right hand side. 5078 – originally with a D prefix and later numbered 24078 – was in service from February 1960 to September 1976. Under a thick layer of dirt was a coat of Brunswick Green paint. (*Derek Penney; Richard Thompson/Online Transport Archive*)

In this powerful study, 75048 approaches Dovey Junction with the Aberystwyth portion of the up CCE in 1966. This exposed section hugging the shore of the volatile Dovey (Dyfi) Estuary required regular observation and maintenance. The steps on the left led to the road above and the short length of track at right angles to the mainline could accommodate a plate-layers trolley. Having been designed mostly for local freight work, the Standard class 4s were in some ways ill-suited to the rigours of the CR. They were hard riding and prone to rattling and vibrating. Furthermore, when assigned to goods or pick-up duties, especially if shunting was involved, they tended to slip. However, when well-maintained they kept to the express schedules but lacked the power of a 'Manor' on challenging gradients. Latterly, many were far from healthy and this led to further delays and service disruption. Until steam bowed out, Shrewsbury-based locos worked the final duties. (*Gavin Morrison*)

Dovey Junction, originally Glandovey Junction, stands at a remote spot amidst the estuary salt marshes, an area liable to flooding and with no habitation or proper road access. It was built by the CR as an interchange point between its 'Aber Road' and its 'Coast Road' which reached Pwllheli by 1867. This is where the two portions of the CCE were divided and united. In the first view, 9018 and 9004 head a special bound for Towyn (Tywyn) on 27 September 1958. Organised by the Talyllyn Railway Preservation Society, this tour coincided with their AGM, the London leg having been behind LMS Fowler Compound 41123 of 1925 which made this an all 4-4-0 occasion. In the background are some utilitarian replacement station buildings which had just been installed. As more of the coast was dieselised, this junction diminished in importance. (*John McCann/Online Transport Archive*)

In attempt to drum up revenue, the GWR opened several new stations along the 'Coast Road' including Gogarth Halt in 1923. Although located close to some camp sites, no passengers are waiting to board this four car DMU in August 1972, the suffix 'halt' having been dropped in 1968. Note the basic nature of the structure and the windowless shelter. It was officially closed in September 1985, although the last train to use it was 16 months earlier. (*Martin Jenkins/Online Transport Archive*)

A short distance from Gogarth is the resort of Aberdovey (Aberdyfi). Once a thriving seaport served by a branch line, the town was agog with excitement when the Queen, accompanied by the Duke of Edinburgh, visited the Outward Bound School on 9 August 1963. Complicated, confidential arrangements always surround the use of the Royal Train. On this occasion, five 'Manors' were selected – *Anthony* (7801), *Hinton* (7819), *Foxcote* (7822), *Lydham* (7827) and *Odney* (7828) – of which four played a major role leaving one in reserve, all being given the full 'spit and polish' treatment. Having got wind of what was happening, the photographer was able to record various empty stock movements at Aberdovey. A proud driver and fireman pose in the sunshine beside 7827 and 7828 whilst a concerned policeman approaches possibly to remonstrate with the photographer (it was just after the Great Train Robbery!). When the big moment came on Saturday 10 August, the carriages departed for Ballater (for Balmoral) with all but 7801 taking part in the first stages of this long journey. (*Derek Penney*)

Situated to the north-west of Aberdovey, and just over 10 miles from Dovey Junction, is the coastal resort of Towyn which is home to the Talyllyn Railway. In the first view, BR Standard 2-6-2 Class 3 Tank No 82023, sporting a dirty Brunswick-green livery, arrives with a northbound class K freight in August 1962. This was from a small batch of locos, designed by Riddles and built at Swindon in the mid-1950s, which were used for passenger and freight duties on the CR. Although reliable and with low coal consumption, their limited water capacity confined them to short turns. Engine men also preferred to operate them chimney first. The second view, taken on 15 August 1966, shows the area south of the station with its up and down passing loops, refuge siding, goods yard complete with shed, cattle pens and coal siding. 75009 is heading towards Dovey Junction with a pick up goods. Economically, the Cambrian coast suffers from a lack of heavy industry but, over the years, there have been bulk deliveries of mail, parcels, newspapers, coal, flour, petrol, fertiliser and agricultural requisites balanced by the outward movement of stone, timber, slate, pulpwood, livestock, gunpowder and chlorine. In the past, Towyn also handled inter-regional troop trains bringing men and supplies to nearby army camps. Freight movements were dieselised from 1965 and ended altogether during the 1990s. *(Jim Oatway; Derek J. Lowe Archive)*

The Talyllyn Railway (TR) occupies a prime place in the history of preservation. Built to the unusual gauge of 2ft 3in, the line was opened in 1865 to bring slate down from Bryn Eglwys to the CR at Towyn and run passenger trains to remote communities. Against the odds, it survived until the early 1950s. With abandonment pending, a preservation society was formed to buy and run the line from 1951, the first such scheme in the world. The volunteer workforce undertook track relaying, loco renovation work and coaching stock repairs, but other items were soon purchased. These included this Andrew Barclay 0-4-0 well tank which was new in 1918 and served for the RAF at Calshot in Hampshire until donated to the TR in 1953. After regauging, it was given the number 6 and named *Douglas* after its donor. In July 1960 it is about to leave Towyn for the run to Abergonolwyn. The track and buildings at Towyn Wharf station were in a parlous state when the preservationists took over, but significant work had already taken place in the intervening nine years. (*Bruce Jenkins*)

Since 1865, the loco depot and carriage shed have been located on the outskirts of town at Pendre. In the preservation era, the existing facilities proved inadequate, so original buildings were extended as seen here. On shed is No 3 *Sir Haydn*, one of two locos acquired from the nearby Corris Railway, which had passed into BR ownership in 1948, but not as a going concern. Built in 1878 at the Falcon Works in Loughborough, it has been a willing workhorse on the TR since its arrival in 1951 and recently underwent a major overhaul to mark its 140th anniversary. For more work-a-day activity, a number of diesels have been used over the years. On the right, on permanent way duty is No 5 *Midlander*, a 1941 Ruston & Hornsby four-wheeler, which was purchased and donated by the Midlands Area group of the society in 1957, in whose honour it is named. (*Phil Tatt/Online Transport Archive*)

The scenic charm of the TR is captured by this view No 4 *Edward Thomas* coasting bunker first between Hendy and Pendre in July 1960. This 0-4-0ST was built by Kerr Stuart of Stoke in 1921 and is seen during the period it was fitted with a Giesl ejector rather than a conventional chimney. The designer of this device had offered a free trial to BR and, when they declined, repeated the offer to the TR. It was fitted between 1959 and 1969 before the locomotive reverted to its original design, with the discarded Giesl being placed on display in the Narrow Gauge Museum at Towyn. (*Bruce Jenkins*)

For the opening of the line, the railway obtained two locomotives from Fletcher, Jennings & Co of Whitehaven, both of which are still in stock today. No 2 *Dolgoch* dates from 1866 and is an unusual 0-4-0 well tank, built originally without a cab. It was the only working locomotive when the preservation group took over and is fondly remembered for its service during this period until other locomotives were available, and it could be released for overhaul. In this view, *Dolgoch* has just run round its train at Abergonolwyn and is about to head, bunker first, back to Towyn. The TR also has many elderly items of coaching stock dating from the line's inception, which adds significantly to the heritage experience. For example, No 5, the line's original guard's van built by Brown, Marshall of Saltley in 1866, is still in service today. As a cost saving measure in slack periods, the guard was often called on to sell tickets from the window as well as other duties, rather than having staff at stations. This practice continues today. (*Bruce Jenkins*)

The narrow gauge railway at Fairbourne, on the south side of Mawddach estuary opposite Barmouth, has gone through several distinct phases during its existence. Opened in 1895 as a 2ft gauge horse-drawn tramway to extract construction materials from the foreshore, a few vehicles were also built to convey passengers from the CR station along the shoreline to the Barmouth ferry terminal. In 1916, the line was reoriented as a pure tourist line, its gauge being narrowed to 15in and the first steam locomotive delivered. From the ferry connection, the tracks run along the shoreline before heading south with a stretch of roadside running, giving an overall running length of about two miles. Built in 1961 by Guest Engineering of Stourbridge, *Sylvia* was a petrol hydraulic bogie loco and is seen that September heading back over the dunes to Fairbourne, with Barmouth in the background. (*Phil Tatt/ Online Transport Archive*)

In 1972, motor launch *Britannia* waits to take a few passengers across to Barmouth. Note the very basic gangplank. *(Phil Tatt/Online Transport Archive)*

Seen on 24 July 1973, *Sian* was a 2-4-2 built specially for the line by Guest in 1963. Heavily rebuilt to a 'Wild West' design in 1984, the engine has subsequently been preserved and is based at the Kirklees Light Railway in Yorkshire. Without the long heritage and enthusiast following of many of the other Great Little Trains, ridership declined in the 1970s and 1980s and the line passed to new owners in 1984. They instigated radical changes, resulting in a further regauging, this time taking it into the miniature category at 12¼in, which led to the introduction of new locos and coaching stock. The line continues to operate but has been through some difficult financial times in recent years. *(John McCann/Online Transport Archive)*

Looking down from old quarry workings above Arthog, this pair of coupled DMUs has just emerged from the spectacular section round the Friog rocks in August 1972 and are now running between the salt marshes on the exposed section towards Morfa Mawddach. In the distance is the low sandy spit carrying the Fairbourne Railway. Until 18 January 1965, Morfa Mawddach served as junction for the line from Ruabon. As detailed earlier, flooding during the night of 11/12 December 1964 had put the middle section of this line out of action. Furthermore, as the route was listed for closure in mid-January 1965, the breach was not repaired although rail services continued either side of the floods between Ruabon and Llangollen, as seen earlier, and Barmouth and Corwen. (*Martin Jenkins/Online Transport Archive*)

Corwen was the most important intermediate station on the 54½ mile line from Ruabon to Barmouth and the junction for the former L&NWR line from Rhyl. In its heyday, this small market town had a loco shed, turntable, large goods yard, cattle dock and loops enabling passenger trains to overtake slower moving freights. During the inter-war years, passenger traffic had declined so, on the outbreak of war, a reduced weekday only service was introduced. Both these views were taken following the floods of December 1964. In the first, the fireman has the bag in the tank whilst the driver of the Mogul 2-6-0 waits to turn off the supply before heading westwards, bunker first, on a pick up goods, on this occasion mostly mineral wagons. Note the delicate shape of the platform awning and supply of slack to feed the brazier to keep the water from freezing during the winter months. In the second, 'Dukedogs' 9021 and 9017 have just been replenished and are about to depart for Minffordd on the Cambrian 'Coast Road' on 26 April 1958. They are double-heading a Festiniog Railway Society AGM Special and can be seen again on page 121. (*Dave Southern; Derek Penney*)

When the Ruabon-Barmouth line was closed, Crosville became the principal beneficiary, with three services connecting Wrexham and Barmouth (D93, D94 and limited stop L61) plus some inter-linked services to smaller villages. Here, coach-seated Bristol SC CSG658 is seen outside Corwen Station with a D93. The SC was Crosville's principal vehicle type for operating some of its most rural Welsh routes at the time, with 79 of the type entering service between 1957 and 1961. It has a front-mounted Gardner 4LK engine with the driver sitting alongside, but a full-fronted body to give a more modern look, although having the bonnet inside the saloon created a noisy atmosphere for passengers. Despite this rather archaic layout, the type remained in service until 1976. After being withdrawn in 1973, CSG658 spent a further six years with an independent in North East Wales. *(Anthony Drewry)*

Many smaller villages in Wales had very sparse service patterns, with only a handful of buses per day. One such is the attractive village of Llandrillo, west of Corwen but off the main road, and which was served only by the D94 variant of the through Barmouth-Wrexham service. In this view, dual-purpose Bristol RE ERG272 is crossing the River Ceidiog, a tributary of the Dee. Dating from 1973, the bus passed to Crosville Wales with the splitting of the company and survived until 1987, before seeing service with operators in the North West of England. *(Dennis Kerrison)*

Moving westwards to Bala with a view looking towards Bala Junction on the 30 March 1959. Pannier 7428 has arrived from Blaenau Ffestiniog and will soon leave for the Junction whilst 8727 is at the down platform. On the left is the signal box, turntable and single road loco shed complete with overhead water tank which were closed when the service to the Junction was abandoned on 16 January 1965. On the right is a grand castellated goods shed built to appease a local landowner opposed to construction of the railway. Swindon-built Pannier tank 8727 was in traffic from December 1930 to April 1962. The rugged, mountainous line to Blaenau was one of the bleakest, most challenging in the country especially during the winter when blizzards and snow drifts often buried the track. Things became distinctly frosty when the heating failed in the carriages as one of the authors can testify. (*Gavin Morrison*)

Located a short distance to the south-east was Bala Junction, an isolated station on the Ruabon-Barmouth line. In 1962, an unidentified Pannier tank with a single carriage departs for its five minute run to Bala from the north side of the island platform. This housed the station buildings and trains for Ruabon departed from its south face. Also on view are the signal box, bracket signals, water tower, water columns, footbridge, token catchers and pagoda style waiting room on the down platform. Following abandonment of the service to Blaenau Ffestiniog, the name-board was repainted and stated 'Bala Junction change for Bala'. The last service trains passed through here on 16 January 1965. (*David Waldren*)

Knowing the truncated Corwen-Barmouth service was about to close, some photographers braved the elements to record activity during its dying days. Although traffic was never heavy, it had been well used by goods trains during both wars as well as by summer Saturday specials making for the coast. When it was actively promoted as the line through the 'British Tyrol' and 'Through the Marches and the Dee Valley to the sea' this led to a surge in seasonal traffic. To ensure maximum occupancy, additional passing loops were provided including this one at Llanuwchllyn where 46446 and 41204 are seen on 19 December 1964. The driver of the up train is ready to hand the single line token to the signalman who will then reissue it to the engine men on 46446 allowing it to proceed towards Barmouth. The main station building was on the up platform which also had a signal box and beyond that a cattle dock, warehouse and a loop for accommodating goods trains. Water columns were located on both platforms. (*Gavin Morrison*)

An early addition to the ranks of the Great Little Trains of Wales was the Bala Lake Railway. Built on a short section of the Ruabon-Barmouth line, laid to a gauge of 600mm (1ft 11⅝in) and opened to the public in 1972, its base is at Llanuwchllyn (seen here), where some of the original buildings have survived. Extensions have taken the line east to Penybont, some 4½ miles away. Ambitious plans also exist to bridge the River Dee in order to access Bala town centre. The railway has a significant number of 'Quarry Hunslets', but in service almost from the start of operations has been *Merionnydd*, a Bo-Bo diesel built by Severn Lamb in 1973 to loosely resemble the BR Westerns. (*Harry Luff/Online Transport Archive*)

Another loop, complete with signal box, opened at Garneddwen near the summit of the line in 1913. The short platforms added in 1928 are just visible in the background as 41204 storms past with a down train on 19 December 1964 by which time the loop and signal box were disused. From here the line descended steeply into Dolgellau. On this particular day, three locos, 41204, 41241 and 46446, maintained the reduced service. (*Gavin Morrison*)

Having worked up the bank from Dolgellau with grades as steep as 1-in-50, 41241 powers into Drws-y-Nant on a bitterly cold 19 December 1964 with a two coach stopping train to Corwen. Here, road, rail and river were in close proximity. On summer Saturdays, signal men would have worked hard controlling movements through this strategic passing loop and walking down to the platforms to receive and deliver the single track tokens. Although, many stations were equipped with token catchers, most had fallen into disuse. Note the classic GWR name-board and store shed. Also visible is the track accessing a former cattle dock. Built at Crewe in 1949, this loco passed into preservation after it was withdrawn in December 1966. (*Gavin Morrison*)

In the first view taken in September 1961, 46446 enters Bontnewydd station which was located on a long descent from Garneddwen to Dolgellau. Originally single track, a passing loop was added in 1923 together with a new platform, seen on the right, which backed onto the River Wnion. The main station building was on the opposite side. The second view was taken in August 1962 at Dolgellau (Dolgelley until September 1960). Having just arrived with a service from Barmouth, BR Standard Class 2 No 78002 will uncouple, run round and eventually return tender first. Designed for light passenger work, this 2-6-0 had recently replaced Pannier tanks on this shuttle which operated approximately four times a day taking 27 minutes to cover the 9 miles. 78002 was withdrawn for scrap in June 1966. During the floods of 11/12 December 1964, the station was swamped but staff succeeded in re-opening the section two days later despite knowing the 'Barmouth Road' 'was to close within weeks. However, the shuttles did not run again. This only heightened local feeling with many opposed to the abandonment. The planned closure date of 23 November 1964 was postponed due to problems over providing replacing buses. Hopes that the newly elected Labour Government would reverse the closure were swiftly dashed. (*Phil Tatt/Online Transport Archive; Jim Oatway*)

An internal GWR report described the section through Penmaenpool to Barmouth Junction as 'one of the most enchanting in the world, giving views of sea, river and mountains'. On 20 June 1959, Pannier tank No 7405 drifts past the George Hotel, which is still open today, as it approaches Penmaenpool at the head of one of the shuttles from Dolgelley. In the distance is the small two road CR engine shed which closed in January 1965. In effect, this was really the shed for Barmouth as it housed banking and pilot engines as well as those diagrammed for the 'Barmouth Road'. Built at Swindon in 1936, 7405 was withdrawn in December 1963. (*John Langford*)

The first view, taken in August 1962, depicts 'Barmouth Road' regular, 46446, gliding into Morfa Mawddach station. Opened in 1865 as Barmouth Junction and renamed in June 1960, it was a triangular junction, in a remote location; the triangle being used to turn locomotives. At this time, it hosted three camping coaches and had four platforms, a substantial station building and refreshment room. Now, it is an unstaffed, single platform halt where trains stop on request. In the second view another Ivatt 2-6-0 drifts across Barmouth Bridge, first opened in 1867 and subsequently upgraded. Here, the train is on the long timber trestle and, on the left, are the spans at the Barmouth side, which include an opening giving access to the upper reaches of the river. Strict procedures governed the opening and closing of this swing bridge section. Despite being strengthened to allow for the use of heavier locomotives, by the early 1980s, the timbers had weakened and everything but DMUs were banned. Fortunately, this magnificent Grade II* Listed structure was later repaired. (*Jim Oatway; Derek Penney*)

In the first of two views on the Barmouth side of the estuary, a two coach Dolgellau shuttle has just come off the bridge on 14 August 1955 and has crossed the lifeboat slipway whilst in the second, 5050 makes for the bridge on 31 August 1973 with a pick up goods as it crosses Old Chapel Viaduct which had replaced an earlier worn out timber structure in the 1950s. The BR Type 2 had lost its D prefix and is in BR blue. It was in traffic from November 1959 to October 1975. Amongst the various wagons are some of the distinctive round-topped gunpowder vans which would have been attached at Penrhyndeudraeth. (*R.W.A. Jones/ Online Transport Archive; Derek A. Lowe*)

A stunning overview of Barmouth, its harbour and railway. This was another small coastal town to benefit from the coming of the railway and the subsequent expansion of the lucrative holiday trade. Its two mile promenade running behind the sandy beach was once traversed by the Crosville 'toastracks'. (*R.W.A. Jones/Online Transport Archive*)

These 'toastracks' proved extremely popular during the season. The concept had reached the company when it acquired five such vehicles from Brookes Brothers (White Rose) of Rhyl in 1930. Crosville subsequently bought two batches of three each in 1931 and 1938, the latter being numbered U12-14. These Shelvoke & Drewry vehicles were designated Low Freighter and had bespoke 32-seat streamline bodywork built by ECW. Originally equipped with four-cylinder petrol engines positioned under the driver's seat, they were refitted with Bedford six-cylinder units and larger radiators in 1955, giving them a distinctive snout. U14 is seen on the coast road approaching the boarding point for the cross harbour ferry. When withdrawn at the end of the 1960 season, Crosville's 'toastrack' era came to an end. (*Dennis Kerrison*)

This parking area near Barmouth station, with its stone buildings on Jubilee Road and the dominating tower of St John's Church, provided a good backdrop for the bus photographer. Here, Crosville EUG335, an ECW-bodied Bristol LS6G dating from 1956, has just arrived from Dolgellau on 16 July 1965. This was one of 47 of this early design of underfloor-engined bus delivered in the period 1952-56, but only ten (plus a rebuild) had the bus-style bodywork. This batch was withdrawn in 1970/71 and although this particular vehicle survived into the mid-1970s with contractors, it was eventually scrapped, a fate which befell all other Crosville examples of the type. (*C.L. Caddy*)

Barmouth was the most important intermediate station on the 'Coast Road' where some trains from both directions terminated. Facilities for servicing and turning locomotives were on the north side along with some sidings where Collett 0-6-0 'class 2251' No 2244 of 1945 is shunting in late September 1958. Looking very clean, it has a red painted number plate and the BR lion and wheel emblem on the tender. It was withdrawn in June 1965, the year after Barmouth goods yard was closed. In fact, the whole line was under threat in the 1960s as traffic declined and costs continued to rise. An advance notice of closure was posted in January 1970, which prompted the formation of the Cambrian Coast Line Action Group. Their active and vociferous protests won the day and this highly scenic stretch of line remains open, albeit on a much-reduced scale. (*Derek Penney*)

A truly remarkable view of a former Cambrian Railways 'class 89' 0-6-0, one of 15 delivered between 1903 and 1915. In many ways, they resembled the GWR Deans Goods and were stalwarts on the CR working both goods and passenger trains. When taken over by the GWR in 1923 they became 'class 15', with 11 passing to BR in 1947. Here 892, which was built by Beyer Peacock in 1903, is on an up stopper at Harlech in February 1941. Who took this precious photo and how did he access colour film at the height of the war? This loco was withdrawn in April 1953 and the last class members in September 1954. (*Photographer unknown/ Colour-Rail.com*)

Two further views of Harlech station, which was the only crossing point between Barmouth and Porthmadog (Portmadoc until 1965). In the first, 6395 is overlooked by the imposing castle as it waits to depart with a northbound train in August 1962. This was one of the large class of mixed-traffic 'Moguls' which enjoyed a long association with the 'Coast Road'. This one was built by Robert Stephenson and was in service from December 1921 to November 1964. The second view taken from the castle ramparts, shows the nature of the surrounding terrain, as passengers, mostly holiday-makers, pour off a down train double-headed by 75005 and 75060. Note the contrast between the station buildings on the up and down platforms. The small goods yard, which closed in 1964, had cattle pens and a coal siding. *(Jim Oatway; Arthur Staddon)*

The first view taken in July 1964 shows the goods yard at Penrhyndeudraeth with some of the special gunpowder vans needed for transporting products from the nearby Cooke's Explosives Factory, which at this time was the major supplier to the coal industry. Sometimes, the daily pick-up freight could collect up to 30 loaded vans. When Barmouth Bridge was under threat, this traffic was taken by road to a new railhead on the former GWR line at Maentwrog Road for onward transportation via the Conway Valley, an arrangement which continued until Cooke's closed in the mid-1990s. From Penrhyndeudraeth, the demanding 1-in-65 gradient towards Minffordd sometimes required the use of a pilot engine. Furthermore, the station was at the tail end of a tight reverse curve. Also, great care had to be taken in both directions with guards pinning down brakes on unfitted vehicles prior to descending the 1-in-50 gradient. The exchange sidings with the adjacent narrow gauge Ffestiniog Railway (FR) at Minffordd had closed in August 1946. Some ten years later, part of this remarkable line was re-opened as far as Minffordd. Then on 5 April 1958 it was further extended to Tan-y-Bwlch. To mark this event, the FR organised a tour from London on 26 April 1958 so enthusiasts could ride the new section. Another view of this double-headed special appears on page 108. *(Derek A. Lowe; Derek Penney)*

Between 1808 and 1811, the construction of a substantial sea wall known as Traeth Mawr embankment or 'The Cob', across the mouth of the River Glaslyn created an area of reclaimed land to the east. This was used for agricultural purposes, whilst also creating a harbour alongside, in which the port and town of Portmadoc began to develop. Inextricably linked were the growth in the slate industry and the opening of the FR, whose final stretch into the town is the straight elevated line across The Cob. A toll road at a slightly lower level provided vehicular access, and indeed was the only route from the east until the opening of the bypass road to the north in 2011. Looking north, this August 1962 view shows the FR on the left, including the junction into Boston Lodge works, and an early morning mist blowing in off Cardigan Bay. At first glance the convoy of buses appear to be Crosville, but although the leading vehicle still carries their Tilling green and cream livery, it had been sold in 1959. In those days, Crosville would never have had such a casually-dressed driver! New in 1949 and latterly numbered DKB293, the vehicle is a Bristol K6B with 53-seat lowbridge body and was being operated by Atomic Power Constructions, the contractors for several power stations around Britain, and is heading for Trawsfynydd. On completion of the civil engineering work, these staff buses were sold for scrap. (*Ron Fisher*)

The 14 mile, 1ft 11½in gauge FR opened in 1836, its primary purpose being to transport slate and granite from quarries at Blaenau Ffestiniog to the port located at the northern end of The Cob. With no adverse gradients, movements to the port were by gravity whilst in the opposite direction horse-power was required. Steam was introduced in 1863, followed two years later by a passenger service. *Blanche* was one of a pair of 0-4-0 'Mainline' Hunslets which were bought in the early preservation years from the Penrhyn Quarry Railway. Here, it has just departed from Porthmadog on the ¾ mile journey across The Cob. The loco was later rebuilt with a leading pony truck to become a 2-4-0. (*Phil Tatt/Online Transport Archive*)

Although its primary business was freight, the FR was the first narrow gauge line in Britain to carry passengers, somewhere around 1850. As the quarrying industries declined, so did the fortunes of the railway, with passenger operations ceasing at the start of the Second World War and freight in 1946. However, owing to a curious feature of its enabling Act of Parliament, there was no facility to formally close or dismantle the railway, which gave enthusiasts a golden opportunity to develop a plan to buy the abandoned line, which they did in 1954, assisted by Alan Pegler, who would later go on to achieve fame as the owner of *Flying Scotsman*. The line was gradually reopened from Porthmadog and services reached Tan-y-Bwlch in 1958. In this view, *Linda*, the second of the former Penrhyn 0-4-0s, is seen in July 1970 after it had been rebuilt with a pony truck. (*Phil Tatt/Online Transport Archive*)

This image clearly shows the layout of the FR's unusual Double Fairlie 0-4-4-0T articulated locomotives, the first of which was delivered in 1869, although this one was built at Boston Lodge Works in 1886. Originally named *Livingston Thompson*, it was renamed *Taleisin* in 1932, the name it carries in this July 1960 photograph. The following year it was renamed *Earl of Merioneth* which it kept until a brand-new locomotive carrying this name was built, at which point it reverted to *Livingston Thompson*. It was last steamed in 1971 and, after a long period where a rebuild to operational order was considered, it was decided to undertake a cosmetic restoration instead, and to place it loan to the National Railway Museum in York. It is seen at Whistling Curve, a horseshoe bend about half a mile below Tan-y-Bwlch. (*Bruce Jenkins*)

This Double Fairlie is at Tan-y-Bwlch, having run round its train in preparation for the 45 minute return journey to Porthmadog in 1967. The Duple-bodied Bedford coach has probably given its passengers a one way trip on the line, picking them up from the other end, as part of a circular day tour from one of the coastal resorts. The FR was extended from here to Ddaullt in 1968.
(*J.G. Parkinson/Online Transport Archive*)

Above left: **Beyond Ddaullt, the preservation group** were faced with what seemed an insurmountable problem in the form of the Tan-y-Grisiau Reservoir. This was created as a result of the decision by the Central Electricity Generating Board (CEGB) to develop the Ffestiniog Pumped Storage Scheme, which resulting in the flooding of a significant length of the FR trackbed. Claiming that the railway was abandoned, the CEGB fought against paying any compensation, although they were eventually forced to do so after an 18 year court battle by the railway. The northern part of the trackbed, beyond the flooded section, took on an increasingly derelict air, as illustrated in this view at Tan-y-Grisiau. The lower hall of the hydroelectric scheme can be seen in the back left. The line off to the right was formerly the bottom of a rope-worked incline connecting with Cwmorthin Slate Quarry. (*John Worley/Online Transport Archive*)

Above right: **Determined to return to** Blaenau, a volunteer group – known colloquially as the Deviationists – embarked on the ambitious construction of a brand-new line between Ddaullt and Tan-y-Grisiau, a project which eventually took 13 years to complete. North of Ddaullt, the new alignment consists of a spiral formation and a tunnel before rejoining the original trackbed at Tan-y-Grisiau station, gaining 35 feet in height at one point. The new route was opened in 1978, after which work began on reinstating the line through to Blaenau, which was reached in 1982. (*Phil Tatt/Online Transport Archive*)

During the years covered by this book, North West Wales was home to many pieces of abandoned railway infrastructure, none more notable than the trackbed of the ill-fated Welsh Highland Railway (WHR) from Portmadoc to Dinas. It was completed in 1923 but such were the company's financial problems that the last trains ran in 1937. The lines were lifted during the Second World War and much of the remaining rolling stock requisitioned by the authorities. The trackbed, including the dramatic tunnel section through the Aberglaslyn Pass seen here, survived as a monument to the folly of the line's promoters. Everything changed when the FR returned to Blaenau and then turned its attention to the WHR. The rest of the detailed story is outside the timescale of this book but the line from Porthmadog to Dinas, and on to Caernarfon on the trackbed of the former LNWR Afon Wen line, opened fully in 2011. A connecting trip from Blaenau to Porthmadog and then on to Caernarfon is one of the most dramatic and scenic narrow gauge journeys in Europe. (*Charles Roberts/Online Transport Archive*)

Back at Blaenau, the Llechwedd slate quarry, opened in 1846, grew into one of the major industrial enterprises in the town, and remains open today on a small scale. It was founded by John Whitehead Greaves who was also the treasurer and later the chairman of the FR, ensuring strong links between the two organisations. A 2ft gauge railway was employed on the surface levels, steam operated from the late 19th century but from the 1920s using electric power generated on site by hydroelectric means. Twin overhead wires were erected on two levels and three locomotives with double trolley poles entered service in 1926-30. The first of these was delivered new, the other two being converted from earlier steam locomotives. No 4 *The Eclipse*, seen here, was based on an 1899-built Bagnall 0-4-0ST named *Dorothy*. Operation of this unusual electric railway continued until 1967, the year this picture was taken. *The Eclipse*, and sister locomotive *The Coalition*, are now displayed at a narrow gauge museum at Gelert's Farm, Porthmadog. (*C.M. Jackson*)

With the growth of interest in industrial archaeology, parts of the quarry working were opened in 1971 as the Llechwedd Slate Caverns visitor attraction. Old wagon chassis were converted to rudimentary passenger carrying vehicles and a number of second-hand four-wheel battery electric locomotives, of uncertain heritage but built by Wingrove and Rogers of Kirkby, Merseyside, were acquired to haul visitors deep underground into the quarry workings. (*J.G. Parkinson/Online Transport Archive*)

Between the main towns in Mid-Wales, villages were relatively few and far between and this was reflected in both the frequency of service and the extremely rural vistas, which sadly few photographers had the patience to seek out. Mike Cozens was an exception and, on this occasion, caught ECW-bodied Bristol MW EMG426 in the village of Carrog near Blaenau Ffestiniog (not to be confused with the village of the same name on the Ruabon-Barmouth railway line). The bus is heading back to Llanrwst from Cwm Penmachno but the driver has not reset the destination. The vehicle is one of a batch of 12 which were new in 1961 and passed through several changes of livery during their lives. In August 1973 it was in an all-over Tilling green scheme but nicely offset by the additional chrome strips from its days as a semi-coach. The large lowercase gold fleetname was a short-lived device used in the early 1970s before adoption of the NBC style. The entire batch was withdrawn and sold in 1977, going straight for scrap. The narrow passenger entrance and tricky manual gearbox made these buses unpopular purchases for new owners and none of those from the Crosville fleet have managed to survive into preservation, other than a couple which were cut down to towing vehicles. (*Mike Cozens*)

Llyn Stwlan is the upper reservoir of an innovative pumped-storage hydroelectric scheme initiated in 1963, from which vast quantities of water can be released to generate enough electricity to power North Wales for several hours. The dramatic views from the Stwlan Dam encouraged Crosville to run a tourist-orientated bus service from Blaenau. The stretch up to dam itself is on a private road, the bus driver being issued with a key to open the gate at the bottom before embarking on the steeply graded twisty road to the top. The vehicle in use in this early 1970s view is SMG545, a Bristol MW6G with ECW body, which had been new in 1965 and remained in the fleet until 1980, by which time it was one of the last of the type with Crosville. Visible at the lower level is the Tanygrisiau Reservoir, into which the water released by the Stwlan flows, and whose water level elevation resulted in the flooding of part of the Ffestiniog Railway's trackbed, as described on page 125. (*Mike Cozens*)

Returning to the former Cambrian 'Coast Road' which, after the descent from Minffordd, reaches the busy port and holiday resort at Porthmadog from where slate was once exported all over the world via narrow gauge lines including the FR. Since the reopening of the FR to tourists, Porthmadog has been a favourite jumping off point for thousands visiting the preserved line. In the first view taken on 20 June 1959, the 11.50 Pwllheli to Birmingham Snow Hill via Ruabon is double-headed by 'Dukedog' 9017 and Collett 0-6-0 2281, both of which have stopped to take water before tackling the 1-in-50 climb over 'the hump' to Penrhyndaedraeth. The '2251 class' mixed-traffic 0-6-0s were lively performers and ideally suited to the tortuous nature of the Cambrian but needed assistance with heavier trains. 2281, which had entered service in early 1936, was withdrawn just five months later whilst 9017 lasted until October 1960 and was subsequently preserved. In the second view, a southbound four-car DMU is seen at the station during the transitional corporate image period. The front unit, headed by M56353, is still in green but the rear one is in Rail Blue with BR double-arrow symbol introduced in the mid-1960s. The shelter on the down platform is of Cambrian origin whilst the more substantial buildings on the up platform had been renovated a few years before. Note the large water tower on the right and the contrast in station signage. The two-road loco shed had been at the north end. (*John Langford; J.G. Parkinson/Online Transport Archive*)

Passengers wait with their luggage as 75062 rolls into Criccieth station, one of the most noted architectural structures on the line. The town was home to Prime Minister David Lloyd George, whose house had a commanding view of the railway. From May 1965, this was one of a group of stations, including Harlech and Dovey Junction, to become unstaffed. Goods traffic had already ended in October 1964; the bay lines were then removed and the passing loop in 1968. On leaving Criccieth, locomotive crews heading south had to tackle the severe grade on Wern Bank. In times past, a couple of banking engines were available to offer assistance if required. This Standard 4 would require careful handling and skilful firing especially if using low-grade coal. The loco was only in traffic from May 1957 to February 1968. (Arthur Staddon)

The photographer has taken advantage of a room at the George Hotel on High Street, Criccieth to get a shot of Crosville Lodekka DLB737 as it laid over before heading for Portmadoc on a short journey on route R27, which was one of a pair of routes connecting Blaenau Ffestiniog and Pwllheli. In the background can be seen a visiting Duple-bodied coach from Silchester in Berkshire and a Crosville CSG class single decker. Also visible is the Crosville enquiry office which, reflecting the seasonal nature of business in the town, was only open from June to September. As listed in the company's timetable for 1965, it had the telephone number Criccieth 19. Remarkably this attractive little building still survives – as a fish and chip shop. DLB737 was a Bristol LD6B new in 1955, which was withdrawn and scrapped slightly prematurely in 1968 after being involved in an accident. (Arthur Staddon)

During the Victorian rush to the seaside, the small fishing port and market town of Pwllheli was transformed into a major holiday resort with thousands flocking to its miles of beaches although the original terminal station was a little to the east of the present one, which opened in 1909. Eventually, the line west from Afon Wen which was used by both the Cambrian and the L&NWR was doubled. On summer Saturdays, the extensive coaching sidings at Pwllheli were often filled and the turntable at the loco shed was – literally – in full swing! In 1957, 2281 waits to leave with a southbound class B all-stations to Machynlleth, a journey of some three hours, covering 19 stations and 12 halts. In comparison, the Pwllheli portion of the class A up 'Cambrian Coast Express' made just 11 intermediate stops but was only 17 minutes faster such were the demands of the 57½ mile single track 'Coast Road'. *(Donald Nevin)*

For rail replacement work to remote stations, Crosville bought two 12-seat Commer minibuses in 1964. The first of the pair, SCP1, is seen at Pwllheli about to depart for Ynys, a former station on the Caernarvon to Afon Wen line which had lost its passenger service in December 1964. The fact that such a small vehicle could be contemplated in replacement for a train was indicative of the passenger loadings on the latter, but in the event even the minibus proved to be too big and the service was quietly dropped after a few years. Both Commers were withdrawn and disposed of in 1971. *(Bruce Jenkins)*

The Afon Wen-Caernarvon line was single track and had opened in stages during 1866/67. Together with regular passenger trains, it carried heavy freight traffic including coal, stone, slate, general merchandise and livestock as well as a range of summer extras to Pwlheli and Penychain. These included 'The Welshman' which originated from London Euston and included through carriages for Portmadoc. The introduction of Derby-built DMUs in 1958 failed to stem the decline in revenue. In the first view one of these units is seen at Brynkir in 1964. Here, movements through the passing loop were controlled by means of a lever frame located on the down platform and to handle longer post-war trains, the loop and the platforms were lengthened. A little to the north was Pen-y-Groes. As the largest intermediate station on the line, it supported a passing loop, two platforms, a bay platform for trains on the Nantlle branch, a substantial building on the down platform and a granite, brick and slate roofed waiting room (seen here) on the up platform. Its goods yard had coal wharves and cattle pens. Engine men heading south from here faced a stiff climb to the summit of the line before the long descent to the coast. On 30 August 1961, 42599, an ex-LMS Stanier 3-cylinder 4MT 2-6-4, is seen with a freight bound for Nantlle. Built by North British in 1936, the loco was taken out of service in October 1962. This whole site was subsequently razed to the ground and the trackbed converted into a roadway linked to Dinorwic Quarry. The last passenger trains left these stations on 5 September 1964. (*Allan Clayton/Online Transport Archive; John Ryan*)

These rare views of the mile long Nantlle branch date from 30 August 1961. Both are taken from the guard's van. In the first, 42599 has stopped at the level crossing at Ty'n-y-weirglodd whilst in the second, taken on the return trip, the guard is proceeding to lock the gates with the single line token which had allowed the train to proceed to the interchange sidings with the Nantlle tramway. Historically, this trackbed had once formed part of a long narrow gauge slate-carrying tramway connecting Nantlle to the port of Caernarvon, most of which was subsequently replaced by standard gauge lines with the section from Pen-y-Groes to Nantlle being relaid in 1872. Although the passenger service had ended in 1932, excursion traffic continued until 1939. Latterly, a thrice weekly goods survived until operations ended on 3 December 1963, plans to retain the line for moving stone having failed. *(John Ryan (both))*

Most enthusiasts visiting Nantlle came to witness an extraordinary throwback, a two-mile remnant of the former 3ft 6in gauge Nantlle Railway which still relied on horse power. The first view, taken 20 October 1963, shows the deserted passenger platform and station building (left), whilst on the right are the narrow gauge sidings on the transhipment quay. The floor of a standard gauge wagon would be at the same level as these sidings, allowing for easy transfer of coal and the loading of slate, stone, copper and lead ore. The second view is taken looking into the station yard from the east. From left to right are the goods shed, the coal wharf with delivery lorry in attendance, a quarry office with tracks on either side each leading to a separate splay of sidings, a stub end of the standard gauge with inverted rail chairs as buffer stops and finally the water tower. Note the simple point-work with swivel crossing. On this occasion, the wagons have been hauled from the quarry by a tractor hired from a local farmer. And all this was part of BR! (*Charles Firminger/Online Transport Archive; Sydney A. Leleux*)

On 20 October 1963, the line was besieged by enthusiasts when a tour organised by the Stephenson Locomotive Society and the Manchester Locomotive Society paid an hour long visit. As the last horse, Prince, had sadly died, motive power was provided by a David Brown tractor which took the visitors to and from Dorothea Quarry in tightly-packed quarry wagons which had steel-plated bodies and double-flange quarry wheels which overcame most problems with out of gauge track. As the wagons rode loose on their axles, check rails were needed either side of the running rails at level crossings. Here participants progress precariously through the village of Talysarn on their way back to Nantlle. *(John Ryan)*

On 5 September 1960, a train of the quarry wagons is seen at Dorothea Quarry with the horse ready to plod forward on the picturesque journey to the interchange sidings. Sometimes, loads were sufficient to require two horses, each of which was hired from a farmer. After Prince died, all remaining workings were tractor-hauled. Note the small lifting lugs on the corner of each wagon. These were used to attach chains which enabled the wagons to be hoisted up onto cableways. Known as Blondins, these transported the wagons high above the quarry workings. To the right is *Wendy*, a withdrawn Bagnall 0-4-0ST dating from 1919. To the left, and out of view, are two short inclines giving access to Pen-yr-Orsedd quarry. Here the photographer found *Chaloner*, probably last fired in the early 1950s, loaded on a 3ft 6in gauge trailer and ready to leave for preservation. Built in 1877 by the De Winton Company of Caernarvon this vertical-boilered 0-4-0 had originally operated at nearby Pen-y-Bryn quarry. It is based at the Leighton Buzzard Light Railway, where it operated the first train in the preservation era in 1968, and has subsequently made visits to many other preservation sites, including mainland Europe and returns to North Wales. *(Sydney A. Leleux (both))*

Served by trains since 1852, Caernarvon was another place where the railway flourished during holiday periods when visitors flocked to see its castle, narrow streets, harbour and quay but, out of season, numbers dropped dramatically. Over the years, the station was enlarged to include three platforms plus a bay, loco shed and turntable, goods shed, cattle pens and sidings. The first view provides an overview of the south end where the two platforms on the right could be used by up and down trains. Stanier Class 3 40116 is piloting 40078 towards Afon Wen with a special on 22 July 1962. Both these LMS Fowler 2-6-2 tank engines entered traffic in 1935 and were withdrawn in November 1962. After abandonment of the line to Afon Wen, the track from Caernarvon to Menai Bridge was singled in May 1966. Subsequently, it enjoyed two revivals. On 1 July 1969 it was used by the Royal Train as well as many specials bringing those attending the investiture of the Prince of Wales in Caernarvon Castle. The second instance occurred after the line had completely closed, first to freight in August 1969 and then to passengers in early January 1970. However, following a disastrous fire which badly damaged the Britannia Bridge which spans the Menai Straits, the branch was reactivated on 15 June 1970 when Caernarvon goods yard was reopened as a temporary Freightliner terminal from where containers were transported to and from Holyhead by road. This arrangement ended on 5 February 1972. The site was eventually demolished and is now occupied by a Morrison's supermarket. (*Gavin Morrison; Richard Thompson/ Online Transport Archive*)

As the slate trade developed, a stone quay was built at Caernarvon. Then in 1875, the New Basin, later Victoria Dock, was opened mainly for the import of timber but also other general merchandise. A rail connection was also provided. However, the dock was never a real commercial success, although during the Second World War the adjacent Victoria Works was used to train those employed in building vital components for RAF bombers. In 1937, the Caernarvon Harbour Trust purchased the coal-fired, steam grab hopper *Seiont II* (108 GRT) for dredging the harbour and the dock. Built in Northwich by W.J. Yarwood & Sons, it maintained the buoys throughout the length of the Menai Straits and is seen at the Trustees' berth within Victoria Dock in August 1972. When retired in 1978, the vessel was preserved and occasionally steamed but, unfortunately, the state of the boiler led to it being scrapped. However, the steam engine survives in the Markham Grange Steam Museum near Doncaster. The dock now forms part of a marina complex. (*Nigel Bowker*)

Caernarvonshire was another pocket of independent bus operation in North Wales, with many long-standing companies providing connecting services between small villages and the coastal towns. One such was Silver Star, registered in the village of Upper Llandwrog but with its main depot in Rhosgadfan, which had begun operations in the early 1920s. Most of their fleet was bought second hand, and many of the vehicles were of Bristol/ECW manufacture which had begun their days with operators in the Tilling/BTC group. Typical was EDV510D, a 1966 MW6G with 39-seat coach bodywork which was new to Western National and originally operated as part of their Royal Blue fleet. Withdrawn in 1978, it was bought by Silver Star the following year and gave five years' service before being sold for scrap. The location is Castle Square in Caernarvon on 27 June 1980. The rather run-down buildings have since been restored and through traffic diverted elsewhere. (*Charles Roberts/Online Transport Archive*)

Elsewhere on the Square, with part of the castle in the background, Express Motors' Bedford OB AJC41 is seen in October 1969. New to the company in 1951, it carried the coach version of the Duple body, with the characteristic swoop picked out in a contrasting colour on this attractive two-tone green scheme. Its dented panels are probably the result of close encounters with passing vehicles on narrow lanes typical of rural operations. After being sold, it served as a school bus elsewhere in the area until the mid-1970s. Express Motors, which was formed about 1910, ran bus services for many years in parallel with Silver Star to Rhosgadfan before selling out in 1970 and concentrating on coaching work. Under new ownership, it moved back into the local bus market in 1982, ironically buying out Silver Star along the way. It continued until the end of 2017, when it ceased trading after a major financial fraud was uncovered. (*Alan Murray-Rust/Online Transport Archive*)

In the village of Rhostryfan, having just performed a reversing manoeuvre before heading back to Caernarvon, is Silver Star's ECW-bodied Bristol SC4LK 606JPU. This bus had been new to Eastern National in 1957, passing to sister company Cumberland in 1964 and was in service with Silver Star from 1971 to 1980, the year this photograph was taken. Although placed in secure storage by the company in a remote depot at Upper Llandwrog with a view to possible heritage use, the vehicle and premises were subjected to vandalism and arson and the bus was eventually destroyed by fire in 2001. The company continued running local bus services until 2010 when it sold out to Express Motors. Silver Star continues as a provider of coach holidays, now based in Llandudno. (*Charles Roberts/Online Transport Archive*)

In the past, independent operators' fleets would probably have seen the presence of one or more Bedford OBs, the classic bonneted vehicle of which over 12,000 were built between 1945 and 1951. This example is pictured operating for O.R. Williams and Sons of Waunfawr, better known by their trading name of Whiteways, which had been established in 1911. The vehicle, MHU52, was a slightly less common bus-bodied vehicle; note the straight waistrail rather the swooping curves of the coach type. It had been new to Bristol Tramways in late 1949, and was of the same batch as seen earlier in the line-up at Welshpool (see page 87). It proved a good second hand purchase, remaining with Whiteways from 1957 until 1973 when it was scrapped. It is seen in Beddgelert in July 1968, laying over before heading for Caernarvon on the company's main route. Whiteway's ceased operations in 1988. (*Bruce Jenkins*)

Llanberis was connected to Caernarvon by a nine mile branch opened in 1869. Its station sported a single platform, substantial station building, sidings, a goods shed, loco shed, a cattle dock and latterly a camping coach. Despite an upsurge of seasonal visitors accessing the nearby Snowdon Mountain Railway (SMR), the regular passenger service ended in 1930. However, excursions continued until 1939 with some of the 'closed' intermediate stations still being used occasionally. A new halt was also opened as late as 1936. After the war, excursions from Rhyl and Prestatyn were resumed in 1946 but were limited to a single trip three days a week, one of which was for a period named 'The Snowdonian'. The last scheduled passenger trains were withdrawn as from 7 September 1962 and then, two years later, the thrice weekly goods service was also withdrawn. In this view, taken on 4 September 1961, ex-LMS Stanier 2-6-4 tank, No 42489, waits to leave with the 3.30pm to Caernarvon. This Derby-built loco was in traffic from April 1937 to November 1964. The lengthy footbridge provided access to the side of the lake and the SMR. (*John Ryan*)

At 3560ft above sea level, Snowdon is Wales' highest peak and each year over half a million walkers make their way to the summit. For those not wishing to walk, a 2ft 7½in gauge rack railway has been available since 1896, and this option is taken by about 150,000 people annually, although a return journey is not cheap. The line is built to the design of Swiss engineer Roman Abt, whereby a pair of geared wheels on the locomotive driving axle engage with a pair of parallel toothed rack bars laid in the centre of the running rails. A gripper rail is also provided to prevent locomotive runaways. Five 0-4-2T locomotives were built for the opening by SLM of Winterthur, Switzerland and a further four were added in 1923, the two batches being differentiated by the design of the side tanks. From the first batch, No 2 *Enid* is seen propelling a works train not far out of Llanberis in August 1965. The nine degree slant of the loco boiler, to ensure that the water level is always sufficient to cover the firebox, can clearly be seen. (*Phil Tatt/Online Transport Archive*)

Right: **The SMR has always** been concerned with safety, even more so after an incident on opening day 6 April 1896, when locomotive No 1 *Ladas* fell down the side of the mountain and was scrapped. Locos always push their single coach and are not coupled to ensure that any minor derailment does not endanger the whole combination. At the start of the day, a non-passenger train takes water, supplies and staff to the summit station, where a visitor centre is provided. This elevated view of Clogwyn loop, dwarfed by the peak of Llechog, clearly shows some of the footpaths and, in the distance, some of the former quarry workings. (*John Forrester/Online Transport Archive*)

Below: **The provision of three** passing loops allows for an intensive service and three trains can be seen in this view taken in 1971 with the middle one waiting in Clogwyn loop for the next up train to pass. Sadly, the days of steam locomotives wheezing their way up the steep gradients have become less common with the introduction of diesel locos in 1986-92, although an experimental railcar proved unsuccessful, and the unit was scrapped. New battery-diesel hybrid-powered locomotives are entering service and these will further reduce the role of the steam engines, two of which have already been withdrawn, leaving just five in stock. Their loss will diminish the thrill of this particular ride. (*Phil Tatt/ Online Transport Archive*)

From the SMR, across Llanberis Lake (Llyn Padarn) to another narrow gauge line centred on Dinorwic Quarry. This visit begins within the depths of the quarry area itself. Covering over 700 acres and consisting of two main quarries each with approximately 20 stepped levels or galleries, it was the second largest opencast slate quarry in the world. From humble beginnings in the late eighteenth century, production expanded rapidly to keep pace with the growth in building spurred by the Industrial Revolution so that by the late nineteenth century some 100,000 tons of slate were produced annually. Slowly production dwindled although there were mini-booms following both world wars when, after the first, slate was needed for new housing to replace slums and, after the second, for rebuilding war-damaged property. However, the rise in imported slate and the development of alternative roof coverings spelt the end for high-grade slate. Furthermore, transhipment from quarry to port was laborious and labour-intensive. The gauge within the quarry and at the port was 1ft 10¾in ('quarry gauge') whereas the Padarn Railway which linked the two together was 4ft. This double gauge proved inefficient, time-consuming and increasingly difficult to justify in cost terms. For use on the quarry gauge, some 20 red-painted 0-4-0 saddle tanks, with a mix of intriguing names and numbers, were acquired from the Hunslet Engine Company of Leeds between 1886 and 1932. Latterly, it is said no two were alike. These views show *Cloister* of 1891 and *Maid Marion* of 1903 which are believed to be on Bonc Fawr and Pen Garrett levels respectively, the latter being 1500ft above sea level. *Cloister* was withdrawn in 1962 and is now at Statfold Barn whilst *Maid Marion* is on the Bala Lake Railway. (*Phil Tatt/Online Transport Archive; Sydney A. Leleux*)

This remarkable view looking down onto Penrhydd level gives an impression of the height between the different galleries. So much is visible in this scene taken on 5 September 1960. On the left is one of the towers supporting one end of a cross-quarry cable way. These 'blondins' were used to transfer loaded wagons across vast chasms. In the foreground is one of the circular blasting huts where quarrymen took refuge when blasting was imminent. In the bottom right, *Wild Aster* of 1904 is busy shunting. This 0-4-0 was withdrawn shortly afterwards and is now preserved at the Llanberis Lake Railway, where it carries the name *Thomas Bach*. (*Sydney A. Leleux*)

In places, the tracks passed between ravines, clung to the edge of precipices or entered tunnels hewn into the rock. Here, *George B* emerges from a long single track tunnel on the Anglesey, Hafod Owen and Muriau level. Nearby was a loco shed and water column. This Hunslet was built in 1898 and was withdrawn when *No. 1*, no longer needed at Port Dinorwic, had its cab removed and was transferred to this level in the mid-1960s. *George B* is now at the Bala Lake Railway. (*Ron Fisher*)

A superb study of *Dolbardan,* a Hunslet-built 0-4-0 of 1922, heading a train of rock along the Sinc Fawr gallery in August 1965. From a peak of some 3,000 men, around 350 now remained, many of whose families had served in the quarry for generations. The driver may well have spent years trundling back and forth, in all weathers, along the exposed galleries. Soon he would be looking for alternative employment as would 'the boy' who was responsible, among other things, for coupling up, changing the points and sanding the rails. Over the years, the men had kept their sturdy machines in immaculate condition, taking pride in the highly polished brass work; however, towards the end, the little locos began to look careworn. A major rock fall within the quarry effectively ended rail operation in 1966 but a handful of steamers remained active helping to clear the fallen stone. The last to be retired was *Holy War* in November 1967. *Dolbadarn* was one of three sold by auction in December 1969 for use on the Llanberis Lake Railway (see page 148). *(Phil Tatt/Online Transport Archive)*

Built in 1932, *Michael* was the newest member of the steam fleet and is seen here on 11 July 1961 at the loco shed serving the Dyffryn gallery. All these isolated sheds had inspection pits and, in most instances, lifting gear, so most maintenance could be carried out on site alleviating the need for the engines to descend to the main workshop. When they did go, getting them up and down the inclines was difficult so, on occasions, boilers and other components went up and down as separate units. Some levels also had smithies where buckled and bent parts could be straightened out. Located close to most loco sheds and within the main working areas were special cabins, or cabans, where the men sheltered to eat their lunch and brew particularly powerful tea – perhaps with a little something extra – to keep out the cold. In the winter, high winds and driving rain made working conditions fairly atrocious. Sold to a buyer in Canada in 1969, *Michael* is now at Statfold Barn. Note its full length, protective buffer beams. *(John Pigott)*

Two views on Gilfach Ddu level where the quarry offices and workshops were located, which today form part of the National Slate Museum. The Hunslet engines based here had minor differences from the others, most notable being the provision of full cabs on most, as this lower area was less prone to the wild excesses of the wind on the upper levels which could whip a loco on to its side. Their function was to move wagons between the inclines and the Padarn Railway, a role which *Cackler* fulfilled for over 60 years. Dating from 1898 and originally named *Port Dinorwic*, it had dropped down framing at the rear and safety valves fitted to its brass dome. Withdrawn in 1966, it now forms part of the Thursford collection near Fakenham. The second view is of *Sybil*. Built by Bagnall in 1906, this 0-4-0 spent its entire working life on this level and is currently under restoration at the West Lancashire Light Railway. Note the incline in the background. The quarry also had some 20 or so diesel shunters purchased new or acquired second-hand between 1939 and 1949. *(Phil Tatt/Online Transport Archive; Ron Fisher)*

Moving now to the transhipment sidings on Gilfach Ddu level. Here, quarry gauge wagons were transferred in groups of four, consisting of two pairs in parallel, onto to special 4ft gauge transporter wagons, one of which can be seen in the background, ready for their journey along the Padarn Railway. The first view shows the transfer point on 4 September 1961 just weeks before it was used for the last time and the second is of *Amalthæa* of 1886 (formerly *Pandora*) one of the three 0-6-0 tank engines built by Hunslet between 1882 and 1895. It was also a rare example of a UK loco with a dipthong in its name! After the line closed in early November 1961, the aptly named *Dinorwic* (1882) powered track-lifting trains between May 1962 and February 1963, after which all three engines were scrapped, although a water tank and chimney from one still exist. (*John Ryan; Phil Tatt/Online Transport Archive*)

The seven-mile Padarn Railway – officially known as the Dinorwic Quarries Railway – first opened in 1824 as a narrow-gauge mineral tramway linking the quarry to Port Dinorwic. In 1843, it was rebuilt to 4ft gauge and five years later converted from horse to steam. Many quarrymen who lived on Anglesey would use the railway to reach the quarry having crossed from the island on a Monday and returned on Saturday afternoon. In this view, taken on 17 August 1961, a quarryman is demonstrating how his ancestors used this remarkable 'velocipede' which they placed on the track so they could hand-crank themselves to and from work. (*Sydney A. Leleux*)

Part of this line survives as the Llanberis Lake Railway. Initially, there was talk of a 4½ mile circuit using part of the Padarn and part of the BR Llanberis branch but this did not materialise. Instead, track was laid on the former Padarn right of way on the stone-protected shelf of land alongside Llyn Padarn with its breathtaking views of the Snowdon range. The gauge of 1ft 11½in was selected so that any other rolling stock would not require alteration. When the inaugural 1½ miles opened in summer 1971, it was the first addition to the original six Great Little Trains of Wales. Later the line was extended and is now 2½ miles with one mid-way passing loop. In this view, ex-Dinorwic Slate Quarry loco *Dolbadarn* of 1922, which has operated on the line since it opened, is heading a typical three-carriage train. (*Phil Tatt/Online Transport Archive*)

The single track railway terminated at Pen Scions where the top of the 1250ft Port incline was housed in the building in the background. Also visible are some transporter wagons and a half-width guard's van. From here, the loaded narrow gauge wagons made their descent to the port whilst empty wagons were returned to the quarry. The second view shows the rope-hauled incline which had a mean grade of 1-in-4½ during its 286ft descent. Both views were taken in June 1961. *(Ron Fisher (both))*

Arriving at the foot of the incline, narrow gauge locos now took the wagons to the various sidings within Port Dinorwic, known now as Y Felinheli. One loco engaged here for many years was *No. 1* which was built by Hunslet in 1922. It would end its days, minus cab, working within the quarry until withdrawn in 1967. Now carrying its original name *Lady Joan,* it is at the Bredegar and Wormshill Railway. The second scene taken in June 1961 provides an excellent overview of the port. A BR ex-LMS 'Jinty' 0-6-0 tank engine is about to cross a narrow gauge track feeding into one group of sidings. Everywhere there are stacks of slate ready to be loaded onto ships, lorries and standard gauge railway wagons. Latterly, the quarry company was reliant on fulfilling orders from France but, when these dried up in July 1969, the quarry closed on 22 August by which time only three diesel shunters were still active. Under-investment, new markets, short-sightedness, falling demand and out-dated equipment, all contributed to decline at Dinorwic. (*Ron Fisher (both)*)

Another view of the port. At the end of the eighteenth century, the inner part of a creek was transformed into a quay and tidal dock for handling the growing export of slate. As demand increased, the site was expanded in 1897-1902 when a new dry dock was also provided. Following the decline in the slate trade and the closure of the rail links, other commercial activity also fell away until today the facilities are mainly used by leisure craft. On 8 August 1975, the motor grab hopper dredger *Sand Swallow II* (222 GRT) is in the dry dock. When built in 1947 by Yarwood & Sons of Northwich for Lever Brothers (later Unilever Merseyside Ltd) of Port Sunlight, it was coal fired but had been fitted with a Caterpillar diesel engine in 1963. She was 105ft long and 24ft 4in in the beam. As its mast could be lowered the vessel was able to pass under a main road in order to dredge right up to Lever's Port Sunlight Factory. It was sold in 1981 and eventually broken up in 2003. (*Nigel Bowker*)

Purple Motors and Deiniolen Motors were very closely linked for much of their existence, although they were always to remain separate entities. The former had been formed by Thomas John Roberts in Bethesda in 1914 from where its main service ran into Bangor by two slightly different routes. Guy Arab III JC8427, fitted with a 56-seat body by Massey Brothers of Wigan, was new 1947 and delivered in the company's attractive ruby red and cream livery. It was Purple Motors' first double decker and the only such vehicle in the fleet for the 20-year period until it was sold to a Dunstable operator. It is seen here at the Bethesda terminus of the route. After the death of Mr Roberts in 1941, followed by his widow in 1952, ownership passed to their executors, led by their daughter Mrs Ellen Pritchard. She engaged the owner of Deiniolen Motors, Tom Davies, to manage the company in exchange for his vehicles being able to use the better Purple Motors engineering facilities, an arrangement which continued until the early 1980s. (*Harry Luff/Online Transport Archive*)

Purple Motors' service used the trunk A5 road for part of its route, including this twisty section at Halfway Bridge, just north of Bethesda. The company had an extremely varied fleet over the years, including some unusual purchases, but they were on pretty safe ground with DHD194, a Park Royal-bodied AEC Reliance, which was new to Yorkshire Woollen District in 1959, passed to Purple Motors in 1968 and ran for them until the mid-1970s. The car drivers behind would probably be cursing the bus for causing delays on this major road but were no doubt relieved when it turned off to complete its journey into Bethesda. After a number of reorganisations of ownership, Purple Motors sold out to Arriva Cymru (successor to Crosville Wales) in 1998. (*Alan Murray-Rust/Online Transport Archive*)

Deiniolen Motors was formed in the 1920s and based in its eponymous village, its main route being from Bangor to Deiniolen, with many journeys being extended to Dinorwic. The business was taken over by Tom Davies in 1947 and his subsequent role in managing Purple Motors, and the resulting informal links between the two companies, has already been explained. Deiniolen was a small operation, with the fleet rarely numbering more than two or three vehicles. A long-serving member of the fleet was FCK844, a Leyland Tiger Cub with Saunders Roe bodywork built not far away in the Anglesey town of Beaumaris and delivered new to Ribble in 1954. Passing to Deiniolen in 1969, this 26-year-old veteran was still in daily service when photographed at the Dinorwic terminus on 27 June 1980. The 207 displayed as a route number was actually Purple Motors' telephone number, although technically by this time it should have shown 600207! On withdrawal in 1982, the bus was sold for preservation and has been restored to its original Ribble livery. (*Charles Roberts/Online Transport Archive*)

The small villages around the slate quarrying areas were hit badly when the local industry, and the economy in general, went into recession in the 1970s. Inhabitants were very reliant on bus services, particularly into Bangor and Caernarvon, for their livelihoods. With a scarred landscape as a backdrop, Crosville SNL671, a B-series Leyland National of 1979, runs through the village of Deiniolen on route N93 to Caernarvon on 27 June 1980. This variant of the ubiquitous National was more basic in nature than the original type, the most visible external difference being the elimination of the characteristic saloon heating pod at the rear. The majority of the company's 85 B-series vehicles were allocated to Welsh depots and hence passed to the Crosville Wales at the split in 1986. Like many Leyland Nationals, it would go on to have a number of small operator owners. (*Charles Roberts/Online Transport Archive*)

When first opened in March 1850, the stunning Britannia Bridge completed the vital link between London and Dublin with Irish Mail expresses now being the most important trains along the North Wales coast. This fascinating view of the bridge from the front of a DMU was taken after the fire which occurred on 23 May 1970. The event was a BR Menai Bridge Preview Special held on 30 January 1972, and the unit is about to enter one of the wrought iron rectangular tubes supported by high stone towers which were at the core of Robert Stephenson's design. At this stage, both tubes were still intact although the west side one had been bent by the blaze. The lions guarding the approach stare stonily ahead as workmen and spectators watch the unit pass by wrong line on the up track. The following weekend, the Wirral Railway Circle ran an enthusiasts' railtour, which also marked the closure of the line to Caernarvon, after which the bridge was closed for conversion to steel open-deck before re-opening to rail and road. (*John Ryan*)

Between 1826 and 1980, the only road access onto Anglesey was by way of Thomas Telford's Menai Suspension Bridge. Once open, farmers no longer had to drive their cattle to market by forcing them to swim across the treacherous Menai Strait. Construction began in 1819, with the erection of the two towers and their associated viaduct spans connecting them to an elevated position on either side of the strait. The towers were linked by a 577ft wooden road deck, suspended from the towers by sixteen iron chain cables. For 200 years, this magnificent structure has hardly changed although the decking and chains have been replaced by steel. Until the opening of the upper level road deck on the Britannia Bridge, local bus and express coach services would regularly be delayed by heavy car and lorry traffic on this trunk route over the suspension bridge, much of which was travelling to and from Holyhead. On 22 July 1972, Crosville ECW-bodied Bristol RELL6G SRG206 is on the mainland side on route N62 from Amlwch to Bangor. New in 1970/71, most of this batch (including SRG206) had been withdrawn before the company split in 1986. (*Peter Jackson*)

Every day at 10.45am between Whitsuntide and September, the *St Tudno* or *St Seriol*, would sail from Liverpool, weather permitting, call at Llandudno and then continue to Menai Bridge where passengers could connect with Crosville buses to Bangor as well as points on Anglesey. After a stop of some 90 minutes, the vessel departed at 3.45pm for the trip back to Liverpool via Llandudno. In the summer of 1956, *St Tudno* (2326 GRT) is going full astern from St Georges Pier at Menai Bridge, with Bangor Pier visible in the background. This was the largest vessel owned by the Liverpool & North Wales Steamship Company fleet. Launched by Fairfields in 1926 she had single-reduction geared turbines and oil-fired boilers. For handling in narrow waters, she had a rudder at the bow. Her spacious decks, lounges and refreshment rooms were popular with the public many of whom made regular day trips from Merseyside. This handsome vessel made her final passenger sailing on 16 September 1962 after which she was broken up. (*Dermot Priestley/Online Transport Archive*)

The first station on Anglesey, Llanfair PG, had opened in 1848 as a temporary terminus before the bridge was opened, a role it was to play again some 120 years later. To entice visitors, the station name was monstrously elongated to Llanfairpwllgwyngyllgogerychwyrndrobwllllantysiliogogogoch, making it the longest in the world. To prevent the much-prized board being stolen, it was removed shortly before the station closed on 12 February 1966. Fortunately, this was not the end for Llanfair PG. Following the Britannia Bridge fire, a temporary station was opened from where an emergency service operated to and from Holyhead usually with a two-car DMU, the trains connecting with buses to and from Bangor. This arrangement was in place from 29 May 1970 until 31 January 1972 when the temporary station closed. However, following local pressure for permanent reinstatement, the original station was rebuilt and re-opened on 7 May 1973 complete with its world-famous name. Now it is an unstaffed halt named Llanfairpwll. With the name-board visible, this short freight of empty tanks is bound the Octel Chemical Works at Amlwch in 1963 and is headed by an Ivatt 2-6-2 tank engine. (*Allan Clayton/Online Transport Archive*)

In the first view, passengers are transferring at Gaerwen onto the branch train for Amlwch on 22 August 1964. Although DMUs took over workings on the single track branch in 1956, steam was reintroduced during the summers of 1963 and 1964 when the DMUs were transferred to other duties. Although most trains originated at Bangor, some started at Gaerwen and were operated by two coach rail motors, the PL and PS on the control trailer standing for pull and push. This was another station to close to passengers on 12 February 1966 since when the station building has been demolished. In the second view, a Derby Lightweight DMU calls at Llanerchymedd during the winter of 1963. There were some eight return workings on weekdays and the trains were reasonably well-used. The access to the station goods yard is visible in the background. On 5 December 1964, the Beeching axe descended and all traffic on the line ended except for movements to and from the Octel Chemical Works at Amlwch. Occasional special passenger trains were operated on the line in later years, the last being on 9 October 1993. (*Blake Paterson; Allan Clayton/Online Transport Archive*)

The Amlwch branch was opened in stages between 1864 and 1867 and was used for the transportation of minerals, coal, livestock, agricultural produce and fertiliser. Although general freight had declined after the war, the opening of a Bromine extraction plant in 1953 led to the branch surviving for another 40 years as the ethylene dibromide was carried in special tankers until it was deemed safe to transport it by road. On 22 August 1964, 41226 is waiting to leave Amlwch for Bangor. To the right were the exchange sidings onto the Associated Octel internal rail system located on the north edge of the town. Although the station has been demolished, the 17½ mile branch has been mothballed since the freight finished in 1993, this having latterly operated on the 'one engine in steam' principle. Some optimistic local residents hope that their branch can be revived but in the interim, Llanerchymedd station was reopened as a heritage centre and museum in 2010. (*Blake Paterson*)

Llangefni, centrally located on Anglesey, was the smallest of Crosville's three depots on the island, with an allocation of just nine in the mid-1960s. A decade and a half later, in July 1979, ECW-bodied Bristol MW SMG554 rests on the forecourt between duties. One of a batch of 23 new in 1965, it was one of the few which were not immediately scrapped after withdrawal from service in 1978-80. Instead, it was converted for use as a maintenance support vehicle for the Runcorn Busway, for which Crosville had responsibility, before being used by an angling club in Cheshire. The depot closed in 1989, but the rather rudimentary building is still extant in industrial use at the time of writing. Partially visible on the right is DFB127, one of the last remaining Bristol-engined vehicles in the fleet at the time. (*Roland Williams/Online Transport Archive*)

One Anglesey independent bus operator with a fascinating history was Edward Pritchard of Newborough, or Niwbwrch to give it its Welsh spelling. He founded the company in the early 1930s and it eventually became the last survivor of a dozen or so operators which from 1930 shared services on the island with Crosville. The first view shows SPT65, loading in the heart of Newborough Village. The vehicle is not all it seems at first sight, being a rare Guy Arab LUF with 44-seat Weymann bodywork which was new to Northern General in 1955. It passed to Pritchard in 1966 and was retained in Northern red and cream livery, not being withdrawn until 1984. The second view depicts the real star of the fleet, a 1936 Leyland Cub KPZ2 with Roe 26-seat bodywork, which was new to West Riding. Mr Pritchard bought it in 1949 and it remained in his fleet until 1967, making it almost certainly the last Cub to run in service anywhere. It would turn out on market day or for school services and was often driven by the owner himself until he was well into his 80s. He may well be behind the wheel in this picture taken in June 1965 as the Cub returns to depot. Both vehicles passed into preservation, with the Cub being commendably restored to Pritchard's blue and white livery. The company continued running until the mid-1980s. Mr Pritchard died in 1986, just past his 100th birthday. *(Alan Murray-Rust/Online Transport Archive; Alan Mortimer/Online Transport Archive)*

Another victim of the cuts involving the Chester-Holyhead line was Valley station. Opened in 1849, it had a goods yard and siding serving a corn mill. Later, its station buildings and platforms were upgraded and as late as 1962, new transfer sidings enabled spent fuel from the nearby Wylfa Nuclear Generating Station to be removed. The station closed to passengers and parcels on Valentine's Day a few weeks after the first view was taken of the 9.25am from Crewe to Holyhead on 21 January 1966. Although they had to wait a long time, the good folk of Anglesey campaigned for the station to be reopened and their perseverance was duly rewarded in 1982 although it is now an unstaffed request stop. The second view taken in August 1965 is of the ¾ mile Stanley Embankment designed by Thomas Telford and opened in 1823. Connecting Anglesey to Holy Island and Holyhead, it had to be widened to accommodate a double track railway and, at the same time, a high stone wall was erected so horses would not be frightened by passing steam locos. At this time, the principal departures from Holyhead included 'The Emerald Isle Express' and 'The Irish Mail'. In August 1965, an unidentified English Electric Type 4 heads towards Britannia Bridge. (*John Ryan; Phil Tatt/Online Transport Archive*)

Off the far west coast of Anglesey, Holyhead is located on Holy Island and connected to Anglesey itself by a number of bridges and causeways across the Cwmryan Strait. The best known are the road and rail causeways connecting the village of Valley and Holy Island, as pictured opposite. A few miles further south is an alternative route via Trearddur Bay which crosses a small inlet at the village of Four Mile Bridge, which takes its name from its distance from Holyhead. This less direct route was used by the N45, one of a number of alternative Crosville routes linking Bangor and Holyhead. In this 1962 view, the service was being operated by Bristol LD DLB850, dating from 1956, which lasted in the fleet until 1971 before a further three years' of use by a contractor. (A. Moyes)

Since completion of the line from Chester in 1850, the ancient market town of Holyhead has been the major embarkation point for the transfer of mail and other goods between London and Dublin. Following completion of Thomas Telford's highway in the 1820s, the port grew substantially. Piers and breakwaters were constructed and, by 1880, the deep water Inner Harbour had two passenger berths, six berths for imports and exports, a coaling berth, a public quay and a new graving dock (replacing an earlier one built by Telford). Over the years, these facilities have been used by a variety of railway-owned vessels, some carrying mail and passengers to and from Dun Laoghaire and some transporting livestock and other goods. A handful of ships, representing different epochs, are shown on the next few pages. The oldest of the mail ships to be caught in colour is the twin screw steamer *Princess Maud* (2886 GRT).which was launched in 1934 for use on the LMS Stranraer-Larne service. Its observation lounge behind the forward mast was later adopted by the next generation of Holyhead mail steamers. During the war, it was the last vessel to leave the beaches of Dunkirk in 1940. After serving as a troop ship, it was converted to oil burning and transferred to the Holyhead mail service, a role it fulfilled until replaced by *Holyhead Ferry 1* in July 1965, after which it was sold to spend further time in Greek waters. Seen here in August 1965, it was 330ft long, 49ft 1in in the beam with a draught of 11ft 6½in. (*Phil Tatt/Online Transport Archive*)

Moored alongside a berth on the west side in August 1965 is the twin screw steamship *Slieve League* (1343 GRT). Launched for the LMS by William Denny & Sons, it entered service in 1936 and was fairly typical of the well-proportioned railway cargo steamers of the period. Used for some 30 years on the Holyhead to Dublin, North Wall and Greenore service, it was 310ft long, 45ft in the beam with a loaded draught of 12ft 8in. It was licensed to carry 655 cattle 'on the hoof' as well as other goods, including containers, and remained coal-fired until sent for scrap in 1967. By this time, its mast had been moved forward of the funnel in order to create more on deck space for containers. Its lifeboats were equipped with hand-operated propellers. (*Phil Tatt/Online Transport Archive*)

Entering the harbour on a calm day in August 1965 is the twin screw motor vessel *Cambria* (4972 GRT). Along with her twin, *Hibernia,* it was built for BR by Harland & Wolff in Belfast in 1948, both ships entering service on the Holyhead-Dun Laoghaire mail service in 1949 when they were the largest of any cross-channel British vessels. They were licensed to carry 2000 passengers in first and second class accommodation and were fitted with a range of cabins and berths for overnight sailings. Their dimensions were 397ft in length, 56ft 3in in the beam with a draught of 14ft 10in. To offer passengers a more comfortable crossing, stabilisers were fitted in 1951 by which time the crossings were overnight except during the summer and on holidays when there were also daytime sailings. When this view was taken, both vessels offered 11 different forms of overnight accommodation ranging from a first-class Cabin de Luxe with toilet and bath at £3 per person or £3/10/- for two people, to a second-class open berth with rug and pillow for just 7/-. Also at the height of the season, tickets for specific sailings had to be pre-purchased. In 1964/65, both underwent major refits when airline type seating was installed and some cabin space transformed into improved refreshment areas. Except for a spell at the beginning of the 1970s when *Cambria* was transferred to the Heysham-Dun Laoghaire crossing, both remained as the mainstay of the Holyhead service until sold in 1976. Eventually, the pair were scrapped in 1981. (*Phil Tatt/Online Transport Archive*)

With the rapid growth in containerisation, a large rail-connected deep-water container berth, complete with a long jetty equipped with two travelling cranes and a conveyor, was built around 1970 on the east side of the Inner Harbour. In this view the Sealink container ship, *Brian Boroime* (4079 GRT), which was built at Cork for the Holyhead to Dublin or Belfast crossings, is at the container jetty shortly after entering service. After being laid up at Falmouth in 1979, it ended its days as the *Abdul H* until broken up in 2011. The brand name Sealink was adopted in 1970 after the shipping division of BR was separated from the rail division in 1968. The container area only lasted until 2009 and the site has since been cleared. (*Allan Clayton/Online Transport Archive*)

In this view taken looking across to the east side of the Inner Harbour in the late 1970s, the container terminal is prominent together with tugboats *Afon Goch* and *Afon Wen*. Having just completed the crossing from Dun Laoghaire is *St Columba* (11,690 GRT) which was launched in Aalborg, Denmark, in 1977. This large rear-loading vessel represents the latest development on this famous crossing during the period covered by this book. It was 424ft long, 68ft in the beam, had a draught of 15ft 5in and could carry 1700 passengers and up to 335 cars. After Sealink was taken over by Stena Line in 1990, it received a major refit and was renamed *Stena Hibernia*. It is still actively sailing on the Red Sea as the *Masarrah*. (*Richard Thompson/Online Transport Archive*)

In this overview taken in 1971, the photographer has managed to capture several generations of vessels in one shot. On the left is TSS *Holyhead Ferry 1*, the first vehicle-carrying, drive-on, drive-off ferry which was built on the Tyne by Hawthorne, Leslie and was on the Dun Laoghaire service from 1965 until 1973. Designed to carry 150 cars, it was later transferred to other Sealink services, renamed *Earl Leofric*, and scrapped in 1981. Behind is *Slieve Bawn*, sister ship to *Slieve League*, and fourth in line is *Slieve Bearnagh*, another almost identical cargo steamer. Both were launched in 1936 and converted to oil burning in 1961 with the latter initially working the Heysham-Belfast service. They survived until 1971 with the former licensed to carry 718 cattle and the latter 735. In the far distance is *Hibernia*, sister ship to the *Cambria*. Between the two *Slieve* Class vessels, both of which were probably withdrawn at this point, is *Isle of Ely*, built by Goole Shipbuilding in 1958, originally based at Harwich, but transferred to Holyhead in 1969. It served with Sealink until 1978 and was scrapped in 1984. This tour of the Inner Harbour concludes with a fine study of the aptly named Holyhead-based dredger *Pick Me Up* (170 GRT), which was built as a hopper barge on the Clyde in 1902 and was later fitted with a steam grab crane in order to assist in keeping the approaches to the port clear of sand and silt. It was 105ft long, 22ft 7in in the beam, had a draught of nearly 8ft and was powered by two-cylinder compound engines. Passed to the British Transport Commission in 1948, it is seen here on 22 August 1968 after it may already have been decommissioned. The 67-year-old vessel was scrapped at Portsmouth the following year. (*Allan Clayton/Online Transport Archive; John Ryan*)

Two views of the Holyhead Breakwater Railway, latterly a unique BR outpost. Originally opened in the late 1840s as a broad gauge line, it was totally isolated and built to transport stone from a quarry on Holyhead Mountain for use in the construction of an extensive 1½ mile breakwater, the second largest in the world and the largest in Europe. Completed in 1873, this mammoth Z-shaped structure protects the port. In 1911, a standard gauge line was laid alongside the original track which was subsequently removed. From then on, the 2½ mile railway continued to bring stone to repair and maintain the breakwater as well as transporting supplies to the lighthouse. Eventually, the early steam and diesel locos were replaced by two Andrew Barclay 0-4-0 diesel shunters, D2954 and D2955, which were renumbered 01001 and 01002 in 1973, although the former was not used after 1971 and was cannibalised in the small self-contained depot to keep the other going. The sole working loco is seen in the first view attached to a couple of flat wagons on 30 August 1976. The second view shows the inspection trolley at the far end of the breakwater during the summer of 1969. In the background is the 1863 lighthouse whose light has a visible range of 14 miles, The two nuns may have been offering spiritual comfort to the lighthouse keeper! The mile long section to the quarry was abandoned in 1975 whilst that on the breakwater was last used sometime between May 1979 and July 1980 with both 01s being cut up on site in 1982. All operations are now carried out by road vehicles. *(Barry Shore; John Ryan)*

Following the Britannia Bridge fire, 11 of the 13 locos stranded on Anglesey were repatriated to the mainland. After the bodies were separated from their bogies, they were taken from Valley to Holyhead on a low-loader where they were hoisted onto *Kingsnorth Fisher* by the giant quay side crane normally used to handle material destined for Wylfa Nuclear Generating Station. On 14 June 1970, Brush Type 4s D1724, D1851 and D1940 together with English Electric Type 4, D233 departed for Barrow-in-Furness where they were reunited with their bogies. The 2,355 ton diesel-electric *Kingsnorth Fisher* was built in 1966 and was owned by James Fisher of Barrow. Some stranded Octel tankers from Amlwch and some Freightliner transporters were taken by road to Menai Bridge station where they were re-railed. To the left are the original Customs House of 1830 and Admiralty Arch erected in 1824 to mark the end of Thomas Telford's 'Holyhead Road'. (*Richard Thompson/Online Transport Archive*)

Before returning to the mainland, two further views of Holyhead. The first shows the graceful curving train sheds flanking the 75 room hotel which, together with various harbour improvements, were opened by the Prince of Wales in 1880. Now the interchange between steamer and train is much quicker with passengers embarking and disembarking on opposite sides of the inner harbour. Following delivery of MV *Cambria* and *Hibernia* with their onboard sleeping and dining areas, the hotel was no longer needed and closed in 1951. The building was used for offices until the 1970s and demolished in 1979, and the site is now occupied by Stena House. The container terminal can be seen on the right of this scene taken on 30 January 1972. In the second view, a grimy 4-6-2 Pacific has clearly seen better days as it leaves Holyhead marshalling yards with a rake of vans in early August 1964. This was a somewhat demeaning duty for one of these powerful Stanier 'Princess Coronation' or 'Duchess' class locomotives which had been designed to haul crack expresses between London and Scotland. The relatively flat terrain and slack timings along the North Wales coast hardly challenged these one-time LMS giants. Built in 1938, 46228 *Duchess of Rutland* only lasted two more months. These extensive yards a short distance from the station were shunted round the clock. Until 1966. there was a steam loco shed, turntable, coaling and watering facilities as well as carriage sidings. (*John Ryan; John Worley/Online Transport Archive*)

Back on the mainland with two views of Bangor station which opened in 1848. Although occupying a confined site, there were two large island platforms linked by a stately covered footbridge with lift towers. There was also space for a sizeable loco shed (closed 1965) with turntable, goods shed and carriage sidings. In the first view, hundreds of parcels are on the platform on 20 October 1963. These provided an important source of revenue for the railway. Two locos are on view; 8F 48252 of 1941 and 'Black Five' 45282 of 1936, both of which were withdrawn in May 1968. By the end of the period covered by this book, Bangor was still handling a fair amount of freight due, in part, to the establishment of a cement terminal. The second view shows the approach to Belmont tunnel, to the west of the station, with a Park Royal DMU set departing for Holyhead in the early 1970s. On the right is one of the large L&NWR signal boxes which controlled movements through the station and is still in use today. (*John Ryan; Richard Thompson/Online Transport Archive*)

Just east of Bangor is Port Penrhyn which has a wet dock protected on the east side by a breakwater. From here, slate from the Bethesda quarries went by sea to places such as the USA as well as by rail onto the Chester-Holyhead mainline. In this 29 August 1976 view is the *Stavenes* (188 GRT), built in Bergen in 1904. It was converted from steam to diesel in 1954 by which time the owner was J.G. Kew, hence the 'Q' on the funnel! Eventually, this charming veteran was towed back to Norway and now operates as a working museum steamship in Bergen. Today Port Penrhyn is still trading. It is used to unload sea-dredged sand and export Fullersite, slate dust used for colouring cement. There is also a small fishing fleet harvesting local mussels. (*Nigel Bowker*)

Once linking Port Penrhyn to Penrhyn quarry was one of the most historic narrow gauge railways in the world. A 2ft 0½in gauge line serving a flint mill had opened in 1798. Three years later this was subsumed into a longer line which, owing to the steepness of the terrain, featured horse power, gravity and inclines. As demand for slate increased a virtually new six mile line, eliminating the inclines, was built to the quarry gauge of 1ft 10¾in in 1877/78. The original lightweight steam locos soon proved underpowered to tackle the grades so three 0-4-0 saddle tanks, *Charles* (1882), *Blanche* and *Linda* (both 1893) were purchased from Hunslet Engineering and, except for a short period when other locos were tried, they worked all trains on the Penrhyn Quarry Railway until it closed on 24 June 1962. In the first view, *Blanche* arrives at the port with a loaded train on 30 August 1961. After uncoupling, it will retire to the nearby engine shed as shunting on this level was undertaken by the single diesel loco seen in the second scene in 1958. Acquired three years earlier, No 24 was a 40hp four-wheel loco built by Ruston & Hornsby. (*John Ryan; Phil Tatt/Online Transport Archive*)

Two views of *Blanche* working on the steeply-graded railway which passed through some very attractive scenery. In the first, taken on 30 August 1961, a train nearing the end of its descent crosses a river bridge where the parallel standard gauge track also gave access to the port. This is believed to be one of the oldest railway bridges in the world. To obtain such on-board shots, photographers perched on boards placed between the sides of the wagons. Company officials on site were usually accommodating and, after signing a disclaimer gave permission for enthusiasts to ride the trains and visit the levels within the quarry itself. In the second, the loco has stopped at an unmanned level crossing on 17 August 1961. Note the bucket on the front and also some 'passengers' at the rear. Between 1878 and 1951, the railway had provided company-operated workmen's trains but, unlike Dinorwic, there was no public service and the carriages were crude unsprung, open-sided affairs. Quarry-bound traffic included coal for domestic and industrial use whilst wagons making for the port carried slate, slate powder and Fullersite ground slate granules, the latter in bags protected by tarpaulins. *(John Ryan; Sydney A. Leleux)*

Following on from the previous page, *Blanche* is at Felin-Fawr, also known as Coed-y-Parc. This was the quarry's principal workshop area with some buildings dating from the early eighteenth century. Here, loaded wagons were assembled for the journey to the port, the marshalling being carried out by diesel locos, one of which No 1 can be seen through the bridge. Provided with their own shed, these had replaced earlier petrol-driven shunters. Some also worked on other levels. This one was constructed in 1946 using the frame from one of the petrol locos of which only three remained by 1960. On the afternoon of 11 July 1961, *Blanche* will soon leave the assembly sidings with the afternoon trip to the Port with a cargo of cut slate carefully-stacked into metal-framed wagons which were built by the Midland Railway Carriage and Wagon Company between 1885 and 1896. To the right is the roof of the fitting and repair shop. (*John Pigott*)

The first view of the works area is taken from the bridge seen on the previous page. On the left is the line to the Port. The other tracks lead into the 1903 carriage shed, the 1846 slab mill and the main fitting and repair shops. Note the switches with stub points and moveable diamonds which allowed both single-flanged main line wagons and double-flanged quarry wagons to use the same track. The second view shows some of the stored locos alongside the carriage shed. For visitors, the star attraction was *Kathleen,* a vertical-boilered 0-4-0 built by the Caernarvon firm of De Winton, which had been delivered in 1877 and withdrawn in 1934. On 26 March 1963 it is flanked by two 0-4-0 saddle tanks, *Stanhope*, a Kerr Stuart of 1917, last used 1947, and *Jubilee 1897*, a Manning Wardle of 1897, last used 1955. All three are still in existence. The De Winton and *Jubilee 1897* are part of the Vale of Rheidol museum collection, whilst *Stanhope* is at the Apedale Valley Light Railway. (J.G. Parkinson/Online Transport Archive; Geoff Smith/Online Transport Archive)

A short distance from the discarded locos was a more open area with a mix of tracks and wagon turntables. Note the different types of wagons (sometimes waggons) some with metal and some with wooden sides as well a few basic flat trucks. The quarrymen's houses behind the stone wall survive today. The link between the workshop level and Red Lion level was by means of the Felin-Fawr chain-operated incline opened in 1874. This had continuous chains passing over horizontal sheaves at the top and bottom. In the heyday of the quarry, it was in constant use. On 11 July 1961, two men are manhandling descending wagons, one of which is about to be released from the chain. Although some of the steam fleet spent up to 30 years on an assigned level, they did occasionally come to the main workshop. In the background are the sidings where wagons destined for the port were assembled. When this incline was abandoned, the number of sidings was reduced. (J.G. Parkinson/Online Transport Archive; John Pigott)

The often-windswept Red Lion level was a hive of activity with a maze of tracks and sidings. This was where the bulk of the work was done. On the edges of the quarry were a number of water-balance lifts capable of raising up to five tons of stone in loaded wagons, which were then taken by rail to the dressing sheds where skilled men split it into slates. These were then taken to the head of the incline ready to descend to the marshalling sidings whilst the vast tonnage of waste slate (equal to 90% of all extractions) went from the dressing sheds to nearby tips for disposal or for conversion into powder or Fullersite. A 'regular' on this level was *Winifred*. Dating from 1885, it was from a group of 0-4-0 saddle tanks supplied by Hunslet Engineering. In the first view taken on 28 June 1960, it is outside one of the dressing sheds, most of which had through tracks as well as internal wagon turntables. Whilst the driver took his break in the caban, the photographer was allowed to drive the engine up and down! In July 1962, the same loco is making the short journey to the incline. As at Dinorwic, Penrhyn engines were kept in immaculate condition until their final years. Note the trackside levers for changing the stub points. *Winifred* was one of six engines sold to the USA in June 1965, but is now back in Wales on the Bala Lake Railway. (Geoff Smith/Online Transport Archive; Arthur Sancto, courtesy John Pigott)

Also assigned to Red Lion level were some diesel locos. Looking smart in its lined maroon livery, No 20 was photographed on 26 March 1963. Built by Ruston & Hornsby in 1944 and acquired in 1951, it was one of a number which came from the Ministry of Works. Known as 'motos', these 20hp machines certainly helped to improve efficiency. All but two were scrapped, including No 20 when it was withdrawn in 1965. The small wagon 'tender' at the rear acted as 'a buffer' and prevented locos being damaged by overhanging slates. They also carried chains and other equipment. The building in the background is the Fullersite plant which produced the ground slate granules to fill out bitumen for road surfacing. (*Geoff Smith/Online Transport Archive*)

A dramatic view looking down on Red Lion level in August 1961 where the quarrymen, having descended from their places of work, walk towards the awating Crosville buses. Visible are some of the dressing sheds, thousands of cut slates and (right) some of the eight remaining water-balanced lift shafts installed in the mid-nineteenth century with names such as *Lady*, *Lord*, *Fitzroy*, *Edward*, *Sebastapol* and *Princess May*. Parts of the last two survive today. (*Ron Fisher*)

Two views on Ffridd level. The first taken on 18 September 1964 shows why this was once 'the largest open-cast quarry in the world'. It captures the sheer scale of the operation with the hewn out mountain dwarfing *Marchlyn*, built by Avonside in 1933, one of the last pair of engines to be acquired. After withdrawal, it joined the exodus to the USA but is now back in the UK. Alongside is one of water-balanced lifts. The second picture, also taken in 1964, is of *Cegin*, an Andrew Barclay 0-4-0 well tank dating from 1931. It is seen, together with some of the workforce, outside the Ffridd level loco shed with the men's caban alongside. Sold to the USA in 1965, it even ventured to Puerto Rico before repatriation and is now at Statfold Barn. Some buildings on this level were used to store food supplies during 1942. It is worth noting that following a prolonged strike in the early 1900s, deep-seated resentment still soured labour relations between the men and the quarry owners. However, when these photographs were taken things were far more relaxed. Security was minimal, officials and loco crews friendly and no hard hats or protective gear was required. Visitors were simply warned to seek shelter in a blasting hut when they heard a bell followed by a klaxon which indicated blasting was about to happen. (*Geoff Smith/Online Transport Archive; J.G. Parkinson/Online Transport Archive*)

This visit to Penrhyn ends with views on the upper levels. In July 1962, *Glyder,* complete with cab, is on Twll-dyndwr level moving quarried stone to the incline giving access to the dressing rooms on Red Lion level. Although robust, the sides of the wagons with their double flanged quarry wheels, often bore dents and scars. This was another of the Andrew Barclay locos delivered in 1931. After being sold to the USA in 1965, it was repatriated and is now at the Beamish Museum in County Durham. (*Arthur Sancto, courtesy John Pigott*)

Also assigned to Ffridd in 1964 was diesel No 18. Built by Ruston & Hornsby in 1944 and acquired from the Ministry of Works in 1949 it was the last engine to work on this level on 21 April 1965. In 1968, it was sold for scrap. The driver is wearing a mix of 'civvie' clothes aimed at keeping out the cold. The second view is of *Nesta*. Built by Hunslet in 1899 it was later fitted with an 'oversize tank' by the workshop staff. On 6 September 1960, it is engaged on one of the upper levels. It is believed that the last working steam loco, *Ogwen*, made its final run sometime in January 1965. Both *Nesta* and *Ogwen* are now back in the UK, having initially been exported after withdrawal. (J.G. Parkinson/Online Transport Archive; Sydney A. Leleux)

Back to the coast and the striking section of line round Penmaenmawr were visiting enthusiasts were fascinated to see another vertical-boilered De Winton 0-4-0. Dating from 1893, *Watkin* had been quietly rusting away since 1944 on the Penmaenmawr & Welsh Granite Company transhipment sidings. The general reluctance to dispose of discarded locos and equipment meant that six years after this view was taken in 1959, *Watkin* was privately acquired and loaned to Penrhyn Castle. Today, it is on display at the Welsh Highland Railway station at Caernarfon. The smaller machine was used to transfer ballast into standard gauge wagons. In the second view, 73067 is overlooked by Penmaen Mawr hill as heads east with an express from Holyhead, the carriage slipboards reading 'Llandudno-London'. Designed by Riddles, this was one of 172 BR Standard Class 5 4-6-0s to enter service between 1951 and 1957, this particular engine being in traffic from October 1954 to June 1968. (*Geoff Smith/Online Transport Archive; Dave Southern collection*)

One of the most visited towns along the coast is Conwy (Conway), 'the fortress city by the sea' with its thirteenth century castle perched ominously on a rock outcrop towering over the estuary. Tourists come in their thousands to admire the town's walls and ancient gates, its narrow streets, myriad of fascinating houses and the graceful suspension and railway bridges built by Thomas Telford and Robert Stephenson respectively. The first view shows the waterfront quay. Built in 1833, it was used initially by fishing boats and vessels exporting copper and slate. Since the Second World War, however, pleasure craft have far outweighed fishing boats, such as the one seen here, although fresh fish and mussels are still sold on the quay. At one point the Conwy river, renowned for the depth and speed of its fast-flowing current, was also famous for its freshwater pearls. The second view shows the mighty castle in all its domineering splendour with a DMU snaking beneath. Both views were taken in September 1967. (*Marcus Eavis/Online Transport Archive (both)*)

183

Although permission would hardly be granted today to build a railway in such close proximity to an ancient monument, Robert Stephenson's aim was to blend the railway with its surroundings. This work and the construction of his tubular bridge across the river, complete with its towers with mock-medieval embellishments, cost a staggering £1½ billion in today's money. In August 1965, 'Black Five' 45268 heads an eastbound mixed freight through the castellated arch on the circuitous section of line round the castle. In the distance, through the arch, is Conway station which was on a considerable curve. Much to the fury of local residents and traders, who relied on tourism, this was another of the stations to close on 14 February 1966. After a twenty year wait, a new station with the Welsh spelling Conwy was opened on 29 June 1987. (*Phil Tatt/Online Transport Archive*)

Until 13 December 1958, when a new bridge was opened a short distance to the north, the only option for traffic heading west from Llandudno Junction was by way of Telford's suspension bridge of 1822. From the Caernarvonshire side of the old bridge, traffic was funnelled into the narrow streets of Conway, abutting the castle ramparts, leading to slow moving traffic and inevitable congestion especially on summer Saturdays when huge queues built up on either side. In this last day view, the driver of Crosville KA21, a 1937 Leyland TS7 with ECW 32-seat bodywork, is also contending with two cyclists. It is operating service 406 to Caernarvon, although its single canopy-mounted blind is unable to display this number. The bus would finish service with Crosville the following year before operating with a Liverpool-based contractor. With the opening of the new bridge, the suspension bridge became pedestrian only and is now Grade I Listed. (*Dennis Kerrison*)

Looking from Conway Castle across to Deganwy, Crosville Bristol KSW6B DKB637 heads towards Conway across the new bridge on the short M10 route from Llandudno. The bus entered service in July 1953 and was one of Crosville's last deliveries of this chassis type, which were also the last new vehicles to lowbridge layout. Note that its three-piece destination layout has been reduced by painting over the top aperture. The company's first Lodekka (ML661, later DLB661 – one of the early production versions of the type) had been delivered three months earlier and its inherent advantages quickly rendered the sunken gangway layout obsolete. DKB637 remained in the fleet until early 1969 and ran for an independent in Llanrhaeadr, near Denbigh, until 1973. (*Harry Luff/Online Transport Archive*)

185

This tour round North Wales is nearly at an end. Before returning to Llandudno itself, a couple more views at Llandudno Junction. When the first view was taken on 17 August 1966, steam was enjoying its last gasp. Diesel power was increasingly dominant on many passenger duties but locos like 48252 remained for freight workings. Built by North British in 1941, this 2-8-0 spent some time as a War Department engine in the Middle East. It was withdrawn in May 1968. As part of BR's rationalisation programme Llandudno Junction shed closed in October 1966. After the closure, the former carriage sheds, outside which a Class 40 and a Class 25 are seen in the second view, were adapted to serve as a new diesel depot until 2000. The site is now occupied by a retail and leisure complex, as well as the A55 North Wales Expressway. (*Geoff Smith/Online Transport Archive; Richard Thompson/Online Transport Archive*)

As steam was ousted, DMUs replaced some workings. For example, this Park Royal-built set, a type long-associated with the Chester and North Wales area, is at Deganwy station (1886). Note the bus stop style shelter, tall semaphore signal and the signal box guarding the level crossing. The opening of the station triggered a building boom. On the right is the Deganwy Castle Hotel of 1882, its prominent tower being a later addition. At this time, it was owned by musician Jess Yates who was born in Llandudno and was best known for his television show 'Stars on Sunday'. It is now apartments. (*Richard Thompson/Online Transport Archive*)

Between Llandudno and Llandudno Junction, the railway was paralleled by a series of Crosville bus services. Here, Bristol Lodekka DFG189 has just left the built-up area of town and is heading towards Deganwy on route M11. Crosville's early route numbering was sometimes chaotic and confusing with one number frequently used for many different route variations. The new system introduced in 1959 with area prefixes, allocated the M-series to services in Llandudno, Rhyl and Denbigh. The bus was from Crosville's penultimate batch of back-loaders, new in 1965. Although delivered in the darker 'Tilling' green and cream livery, it had succumbed to the National Bus Company leaf green and white scheme in the early 1970s. Other than members of the open-top fleet, Crosville's last back loaders were eliminated in 1983. (*Michael J. Russell*)

Llandudno was home to North Wales' second curious municipal bus operation after Colwyn Bay. This one was doubly unusual as it was, until 1974, one of only a handful of undertakings in Britain run by an Urban District Council. Operations began in 1928 with seasonal tours around the Great Orme to which were added trips to the Little Orme, Glanwydden Valley and Gloddaeth Woods, all very popular with holidaymakers and day trippers. Although fleet size reached 17 at one stage, for most of its history there were fewer than ten vehicles. Earliest deliveries consisted of small, bonneted single deckers of Dennis, Guy and Commer manufacture, the first of which were of toastrack layout. The last normal control vehicles to be delivered were these two Guy Wolfs with 21-seat bodywork by Barnards of Norwich which arrived in 1949. The pair is seen with several others from the fleet on 20 August 1967, at the Great Orme viewing point near St Tudno's Church on the stage carriage route which began in 1951, probably coinciding with a church service. These two buses remained in the fleet until the end of the 1976 summer season and were subsequently sold for preservation, an outcome which has happily been the fate of a very high proportion of the company's former fleet. (*R.L. Wilson/Online Transport Archive*)

The last two batches of Guy buses were of full-fronted, forward control design, but mechanically quite similar to previous deliveries. CCC596 was one of a pair of Guy Otters with 25-seat Roe bodywork delivered in 1954 and is seen here ascending the Little Orme on Colwyn Road on a town circular service on 27 August 1979. Fleet livery had changed from maroon and cream to blue and white in 1968, but here the vehicle carries the post-1975 red and grey scheme which was introduced after local government reorganisation had transferred ownership from Llandudno UDC to the newly formed Aberconwy Borough Council on 1 April 1974. This vehicle remains in Llandudno, nowadays being part of Alpine Travel's heritage fleet. (*Michael J. Russell*)

Even more idiosyncratic purchases in 1951 were a pair of Foden PVSC6 models with bodywork by Metalcraft of Blythe Bridge, near Stoke-on-Trent. With 35 seats, they were the largest vehicles ever operated by the undertaking, with the exception of a pair of Bedford SBs delivered in 1976. For added safety, their rear axles incorporated sprag gear – an ingenious set of bearings which run freely in one direction but jam on when the rotation is reversed – to prevent run-back on the fearsome inclines of the Great Orme. In June 1965, the first of the pair is heading up the Orme, turning out of Llwynon Road on the edge of the built up part of town. The two Fodens were withdrawn in 1968, after a remarkably short life by Llandudno standards, and did not survive into preservation. (*Alan Mortimer/Online Transport Archive*)

The last buses to be delivered in UDC days were two Dennis Pax Vs with Dennis 33-seat bodywork which entered service in September 1968. These very utilitarian vehicles, on a chassis type more commonly employed for goods vehicles, enjoyed mixed use on tour work and the town service. FJC736F is heading for St Tudno's Church on this steeply-graded stretch of Ty-Gwyn Road running parallel to the tramway in this August 1970 view, during the period when buses and trams shared the blue and white livery. The council was exempted from effects of the 1985 Transport Act because it had so few vehicles, so oddly it remained under direct municipal operation rather than via an arm's-length limited company after 1986. It took the voluntary decision to close down in 1999, by that time in the hands of a new local authority called Conwy County Borough Council, and the equivalent present day services are operated by independents. The two 1968 Dennises survived in the fleet until the early 1990s, with the one pictured here passing into preservation after a period operating with independent operators in England. (*Bruce Jenkins*)

The Great Orme Tramway was opened in 1902 and is today the only surviving cable tramway in Britain. It is technically a funicular, with pairs of 3ft 6in gauge cars permanently connected to each other, with cable houses at Halfway and the Summit. The trams were all built by Hurst, Nelson and Company of Motherwell in 1902. Nos 1-3 were freight cars which lasted under 10 years, one slightly macabre task involved conveying coffins to Halfway, located close to St Tudno's Church. Nos 4-7 are passenger cars with the first two being assigned to the lower section, most of which is street-running. No 5 is seen descending Old Road towards the Victoria Station terminus in July 1960 carrying the very dark blue, heavily varnished livery used until 1962. This section is the steepest on the system, with the gradient being more than 1-in-4. (*Bruce Jenkins*)

Ty-gwyn Road is almost as steep in parts, and also features the lower section's crossing point. Seen on 30 August 1976, 4 and 5 are in the later lighter blue and cream still carried today, albeit with the addition of elaborate lining out. Although overhead wires and trolley poles are visible, these were nothing to do with power supply but rather a telegraph communication between the control room and the tram crews. This feature was replaced by more modern equipment in 2001. Originally operated by a private concern, the tramway was bought by Llandudno UDC in 1948, bringing it into the same ownership as the town's bus fleet. A seasonal operation, it is now owned by Conwy County Borough Council. (*Barry Shore*)

At Halfway, passengers change cars to complete their journey by walking through the depot-cum-station building which is visible in the distance of this view taken from the summit. For many years, the machinery was steam-powered. The upper section, worked by cars 6 and 7, is far more exposed, entirely on private reservation and takes visitors past some long-closed mine and quarry workings. In August 1965, No 6 (right) heads for the top of the Orme, whilst 7 descends towards Halfway. The sweep of Llandudno Bay, the Little Orme and the coast towards Colwyn Bay and Rhyl can be seen stretching into the distance. The views from the top of the Orme can be spectacular, but also virtually non-existent when rain and mist blow in from the Irish Sea. (*Phil Tatt/Online Transport Archive*)

This multi-faceted transport journey round North Wales ends where it began at Llandudno Pier. The first view taken in 1956 shows the entire fleet of the Liverpool & North Wales Steamship Company. Nearest the camera is the majestic *St Tudno* (2326 GRT) and, in the far distance, the *St Seriol* (1556 GRT). Launched by Fairfields in 1931, the latter had twin screw turbine engines, oil-fired boilers and could carry 1556 passengers. Regularly working to Douglas, Liverpool and Menai Bridge, she made her last passenger sailing between Llandudno and Douglas on 6 September 1961 and was sold to shipbreakers in late 1962. During the Second World War, the officers and crew of the *St Seriol* had earned a notable commendation for the role played during the evacuation from Dunkirk when she made no less than seven hazardous Channel crossings. Sandwiched between the two bigger vessels is the diminutive two funnelled MV *St Trillo* (314 GRT). Launched by Fairfields in 1936, this well-appointed vessel had oil fired Crossley engines and could carry 568 passengers. She was in constant use during the season working three short local cruises every day. Following losses due to bad weather and competition from road and rail, the Steamship Company went into liquidation at the end of the 1962 season which led to withdrawal of *St Tudno*. In partial compensation, the Isle of Man Steam Packet Company announced they would make occasional sailings from Liverpool. The second view shows *Mona's Isle* at the stage. With ever-decreasing usage these trips ended in 1980. The little *St Trillo* continued its cruises under charter to P & A Campbell until the end of the 1969 season. Although many of the transport delights seen in these pages have disappeared, there is still a huge amount to enjoy and cherish. (*Dermot Priestley/Online Transport Archive; J.G. Parkinson/Online Transport Archive*)